# The Wadsworth Themes in American Literature Series

1865–1915

THEME 9
*Imagining Gender*

## Alfred Bendixen
*Texas A&M University*

Jay Parini
*Middlebury College*
*General Editor*

**WADSWORTH**
CENGAGE Learning·

Australia · Brazil · Japan · Korea · Mexico · Singapore · Spain · United Kingdom · United States

**WADSWORTH**
CENGAGE Learning™

**The Wadsworth Themes in American
  Literature Series, 1865–1915**
**Theme 9 Imagining Gender**
**Alfred Bendixen, Jay Parini**

Publisher, Humanities: *Michael Rosenberg*

Senior Development Editor: *Michell Phifer*

Assistant Editor: *Megan Garvey*

Editorial Assistant: *Rebekah Matthews*

Associate Development Project Manager:
  *Emily A. Ryan*

Executive Marketing Manager: *Mandee
  Eckersley*

Senior Marketing Communications Manager:
  *Stacey Purviance*

Senior Project Manager, Editorial Production: *Lianne Ames*

Senior Art Director: *Cate Rickard Barr*

Senior Print Buyer: *Mary Beth Hennebury*

Permissions Editor: *Margaret Chamberlain-
  Gaston*

Permissions Researcher: *Writers Research
  Group, LLC*

Production Service: *Kathy Smith*

Text Designer: *Frances Baca*

Photo Manager: *John Hill*

Photo Researcher: *Jan Seidel*

Cover Designer: *Frances Baca*

Cover Image: © *National Archives and Records
  Administration*

Compositor: *Graphic World, Inc.*

For product information and technology assistance, contact us at
**Cengage Learning Academic Resource Center, 1-800-423-0563**
For permission to use material from this text or product,
submit all requests online at **www.cengage.com/permissions.**
Further permissions questions can be e-mailed to
**permissionrequest@cengage.com.**

Library of Congress Control Number: 2008925317

ISBN-13: 978-1-4282-6244-7

ISBN-10: 1-4282-6244-X

**Wadsworth Cengage Learning**
25 Thomson Place
Boston, 02210
USA

Cengage Learning products are represented in Canada by Nelson Education, Ltd.

For your course and learning solutions, visit
**academic.cengage.com.**

Purchase any of our products at your local college store or at our preferred online store **www.ichapters.com.**

We have made every effort to trace the ownership of all copyrighted material and to secure permission from copyright holders. In the event of any question arising as to the use of any material, we will be pleased to make the necessary corrections in future printings.

Printed in the United States of America
1   2   3   4   5   6   7   12   11   10   09   08

# Contents

# Preface

WHAT IS AMERICA? HOW HAVE WE DEFINED OURSELVES over the past five centuries, and dealt with the conflict of cultures, the clash of nations, races, ethnicities, religious visions, and class interests? How have we thought about ourselves, as men and women, in terms of class and gender? How have we managed to process a range of complex and compelling issues?

*The Wadsworth Themes in American Literature Series* addresses these questions in a sequence of 21 booklets designed especially for classroom use in a broad range of courses. There is nothing else like them on the market. Each booklet has been carefully edited to frame issues of importance, with attention to the development of key themes. Teachers and students have consistently found these mini-anthologies immensely productive in the classroom, as the texts we have chosen are provocative, interesting to read, and central to the era under discussion. Each thematic booklet begins with a short essay that provides the necessary historical and literary context to address the issues raised in that theme. In addition, many of the headnotes have been written by scholars, with an eye to introducing students to the life and times of the author under discussion, paying attention to historical context as well, and making sure to prepare the way for the selection that follows. The footnotes provide useful glosses on words and phrases, keying the reader to certain historical moments or ideas, explaining oddities, offering extra material to make the texts more accessible.

Each of these themes is drawn from *The Wadsworth Anthology of American Literature,* which is scheduled for later publication. The first sequence of booklets, edited by Ralph Bauer at the University of Maryland, takes in the colonial period, which runs from the arrival of Columbus in the New World through 1820, a period of immense fluidity and dynamic cultural exchange. Bauer is a pioneering scholar who takes a hemispheric approach to the era, looking at the crush of cultures—Spanish, English, Dutch, German, French; each of these European powers sent colonial missions across the Atlantic Ocean, and the collision of these cultures with each other and with the Native American population (itself diverse and complicated) was combustive. Bauer isolates several themes, one of which is called "Between Cultures," and looks at the confrontation of European and Native American traditions. In "Spirituality, Church, and State in Colonial America," he examines the obsession with religious ideas, some of which led to the crisis in Salem, where the infamous witch trials occurred. In "Empire,

Science, and the Economy in the Americas," the focus shifts to the material basis for culture, and how it affected some outlying regions, such as Barbados, Peru, Mexico, and Alaska—thus blasting apart the rigid ways that scholars have more traditionally thought about North America in isolation.  In "Contested Nations in the Early Americas," Bauer centers on revolutionary fervor in places like Haiti, Cuba, and Jamaica, where various groups fought for control of both territory and cultural influence.

In the second sequence of booklets, Shirley Samuels (who chairs the English Department at Cornell and has established herself as a major voice in the field of nineteenth-century American literature) looks at the early days of the American republic, a period stretching from 1800 to 1865, taking us through the Civil War. This was, of course, a period of huge expansion as well as consolidation. Manifest Destiny was a catchword, as the original thirteen colonies expanded in what Robert Frost referred to as "a nation gradually realizing westward." The question of identity arose on different fronts, and we see the beginnings of the women's movement here. In her first theme, Samuels looks at "The Woman Question," offering a selection of texts by men and women thinking about the place of a woman in society and in the home. Some of this writing is quite provocative, and much of it is rarely studied in college classrooms.

The racial questions came into focus during this era, too, and the groundwork for the Civil War was unhappily laid. In "Confronting Race," Samuels offers a searing medley of texts from Black Hawk through Frances E. W. Harper. These works hurl this topic into stark relief against a cultural landscape in perpetual ferment. This booklet includes selections from the speeches of Sojourner Truth, the pseudonym of an astonishing black woman, a former slave who became a leading abolitionist and advocate for women's rights.

In "Manifest Destiny and the Quest for the West," Samuels offers a mix of classic and lesser known texts on the theme of westward expansion, beginning with the remarkable *Journals of Lewis and Clark*, a key document in the literature of westward expansion and a vivid example of the literature of exploration. She ends with "Views of War," presenting a range of inspiring and heart-rending texts from a time of bloodshed, hatred, and immense idealism. The Union was very nearly broken, and one gets a full sense of the dynamics of this troubled era by comparing these texts by an unusual range of authors from Oliver Wendell Holmes and Julia Ward Howe through Sidney Lanier, one of the finest (if lesser known) poets of the era.

In the third sequence of booklets, Alfred Bendixen, who teaches at Texas A&M University, offers a selection from the period just after the Civil War through the beginnings of the modern period. Bendixen, who presides over the American Literature Association, has proven himself a scholar of unusual talents, and he brings his deep knowledge of the period into play here. In "Imagining Gender," he takes up where Samuels left off, looking at a compelling range of texts by men and women who consider the evolving issue of gender in fascinating ways. One sees the coalescing of the women's movement in some of this work, and also the resistance that inevitably arose, as women tried to assert themselves and to find their voice.

In "Questions of Social and Economic Justice," Bendixen puts forward texts by a range of key figures, including George Washington Cable, Hamlin Garland, Mary Wilkins Freeman, and Jack London. Each of these gifted writers meditates on the struggle of a young nation to define itself, to locate its economic pulse, to balance the need for economic expansion and development with the requirements and demands of social justice. Many of these themes carry forward into the twentieth century, and it is worth looking closely at the origins of these themes in an era of compulsive growth. Needless to say, this was also a period when millions of immigrants arrived from Southern and Eastern Europe, radically changing the complexion of the nation. Bendixen offers a unique blend of texts on the conflicts and questions that naturally followed the so-called Great Migration in "Immigration, Ethnicity, and Race." This section includes excerpts from Jane Addams's remarkable memoir of her time at Hull-House, a mansion in Chicago where she and her coworkers offered a range of social assistance and cultural programs to working class immigrants.

The most unusual theme in this sequence of booklets by Bendixen is "Crime, Mystery, and Detection." Here the student will find an array of gripping stories by some of the original authors in a field that forms the basis for contemporary popular fiction around the world. American readers in this period loved detective stories, and readers still do. The mix is quite unusual, and it remains fascinating to see how the genre found its legs and began to run, through a time when readers wished to apply all the tools of intelligence to their world, discovering its ways and meaning, trying to figure out "who done it" in so many ways.

Martha J. Cutter—a scholar of considerable range and achievement who now teaches at the University of Connecticut—edits the sequence of booklets dealing with the modern era, 1910–1945, a period of huge importance in American history and culture. The American empire came into its own in this era, recognized its muscles, and began to flex them—in ways productive and (at times) destructive. Cutter begins by looking at the women's movement, and how men reacted to certain inevitable pressures. In "The Making of the New Woman and the New Man," she charts the struggle between the sexes in a compelling range of texts, including works by Sui Sin Far, Edwin Arlington Robinson, James Weldon Johnson, Willa Cather, and John Steinbeck, among others. Of course, the subject of class had a massive impact on how people viewed themselves, and in "Modernism and the Literary Left," she presents a selection of works that deal with issues of class, money, and power. At the center of this sequence lies "May Day," one of F. Scott Fitzgerald's most luminous and provocative stories.

The New Negro Renaissance occurred during this period, a revival and consolidation of writing in a variety of genres by African Americans. Here Cutter offers a brilliant selection of key texts from this movement, including work by Langston Hughes and Zora Neale Hurston in "Racism and Activism." This booklet extends well beyond the Harlem Renaissance itself to work by Richard Wright, a major voice in African American literature.

As it must, the theme of war occupies a central place in one thematic booklet. In the first half of the twentieth century, world wars destroyed the lives of millions. Never had the world seen killing like this, or inhumanity and cruelty on a scale that beggars the imagination. The violence of these conflicts, and the cultural implications of such destruction, necessarily held the attention of major writers. And so, in "Poetry and Fiction of War and Social Conflict," we find a range of compelling work by such writers as Ezra Pound, H.D. (Hilda Doolittle), T. S. Eliot, and Edna St. Vincent Millay.

Henry Hart is a contemporary poet, biographer, and critic with a broad range of work to his credit (he holds a chair in literature at William and Mary College). His themes are drawn from the postwar era, and he puts before readers a seductive range of work by poets, fiction writers, and essayists. Many of the themes from earlier volumes continue here. For instance, Hart begins with "Race and Ethnicity in the Melting Pot," offering students a chance to think hard about the matter of ethnicity and race in contemporary America. With texts by James Baldwin and Malcolm X through Amy Tan and Ana Menéndez, he presents viewpoints that will prove challenging and provocative—perfect vehicles for classroom discussion.

In "Class Conflicts and the American Dream," Hart explores unstable, challenging terrain in a sequence of texts by major postwar authors from Martin Luther King, Jr. through Flannery O'Connor. Some of these works are extremely well known, such as John Updike's story, "A & P." Others, such as James Merrill's "The Broken Home" may be less familiar. This booklet, as a whole, provides a rich field of texts, and will stimulate discussion on many levels about the role of class in American society.

Similarly, Hart puts forward texts that deal with gender and sexuality in "Exploring Gender and Sexual Norms." From Sylvia Plath's wildly destructive poem about her father, "Daddy," through the anguished meditations in poetry of Adrienne Rich, Anne Sexton, Allen Ginsberg, and Frank O'Hara (among others), the complexities of sexuality and relationships emerge. In Gore Vidal's witty and ferocious look at homosexuality and anti-Semitism in "Pink Triangle and Yellow Star," students have an opportunity to think hard about things that are rarely put forward in frank terms. Further meditations on masculinity and as well as gay and lesbian sexualities occur in work by Pat Califia, Robert Bly, and Mark Doty. The section called "Witnessing War" offers some remarkable poems and stories by such writers as Robert Lowell, James Dickey, and Tim O'Brien—each of them writing from a powerful personal experience. In a medley of texts on "Religion and Spirituality," Hart explores connections to the sacred, drawing on work by such writers as Flannery O'Connor, Charles Wright, and Annie Dillard. As in earlier booklets, these thematic arrangements by Hart will challenge, entertain, and instruct.

In sum, we believe these booklets will stimulate conversations in class that should be productive as well as memorable, for teacher and student alike. The texts have been chosen because of their inherent interest and readability, and—in a sense—for the multiple ways in which they "talk" to each other. Culture is, of course, nothing more than good conversation, its elevation to a level of discourse. We, the editors of these thematic booklets, believe that the attractive arrangements of compelling texts will make a lasting impression, and will help to answer the question posed at the outset: What is America?

## ACKNOWLEDGMENTS

We would like to thank the following readers and scholars who helped us shape this series: Brian Adler, Valdosta State University; John Alberti, Northern Kentucky University; Lee Alexander, College of William and Mary; Althea Allard, Community College of Rhode Island; Jonathan Barron, University of Southern Mississippi; Laura Behling, Gustavus Adolphus College; Peter Bellis, University of Alabama at Birmingham; Alan Belsches, Troy University Dothan Campus; Renee Bergland, Simmons College; Roy Bird, University of Alaska Fairbanks; Michael Borgstrom, San Diego State University; Patricia Bostian, Central Peidmont Community College; Jessica Bozek, Boston University; Lenore Brady, Arizona State University; Maria Brandt, Monroe Community College; Martin Buinicki, Valparaiso University; Stuart Burrows, Brown University; Shawrence Campbell, Stetson University; Steven Canaday, Anne Arundel Community College; Carole Chapman, Ivy Tech Community College of Indiana; Cheng Lok Chua, California State University; Philip Clark, McLean High School; Matt Cohen, Duke University; Patrick Collins, Austin Community College; Paul Cook, Arizona State University; Dean Cooledge, University of Maryland Eastern Shore; Howard Cox, Angelina College; Laura Cruse, Northwest Iowa Community College; Ed Dauterich, Kent State University; Janet Dean, Bryant University; Rebecca Devers, University of Connecticut; Joseph Dewey, University of Pittsburgh–Johnstown; Christopher Diller, Berry College; Elizabeth Donely, Clark College; Stacey Donohue, Central Oregon Community College; Douglas Dowland, The University of Iowa; Jacqueline Doyle, California State University, East Bay; Robert Dunne, Central Connecticut State University; Jim Egan, Brown University; Marcus Embry, University of Northern Colorado; Nikolai Endres, Western Kentucky University; Terry Engebretsen, Idaho State University; Jean Filetti, Christopher Newport University; Gabrielle Foreman, Occidental College; Luisa Forrest, El Centro College; Elizabeth Freeman, University of California–Davis; Stephanie Freuler, Valencia Community College; Andrea Frisch, University of Maryland; Joseph Fruscione, Georgetown University; Lisa Giles, University of Southern Maine; Charles Gongre, Lamar State College–Port Arthur;

Gary Grieve-Carlson, Lebanon Valley College; Judy Harris, Tomball College; Brian Henry, University of Richmond; Allan Hikida, Seattle Central Community College; Lynn Houston, California State University, Chico; Coleman Hutchison, University of Texas–Austin; Andrew Jewell, University of Nebraska–Lincoln; Marion Kane, Lake-Sumter Community College; Laura Knight, Mercer County Community College; Delia Konzett, University of New Hampshire; Jon Little, Alverno College; Chris Lukasik, Purdue University; Martha B. Macdonald, York Technical College; Angie Macri, Pulaski Technical College; John Marsh, University of Illinois at Urbana Champaign; Christopher T. McDermot, University of Alabama; Jim McWilliams, Dickinson State University; Joe Mills, North Carolina School of the Arts; Bryan Moore, Arkansas State University; James Nagel, University of Georgia; Wade Newhouse, Peace College; Keith Newlin, University of North Carolina Wilmington; Andrew Newman, Stony Brook University; Brian Norman, Idaho State University; Scott Orme, Spokane Community College; Chris Phillips, Lafayette College; Jessica Rabin, Anne Arundel Community College; Audrey Raden, Hunter College; Catherine Rainwater, St. Edward's University; Rick Randolph, Kaua; Joan Reeves, Northeast Alabama Community College; Paul Reich, Rollins College; Yelizaveta Renfro, University of Nebraska–Lincoln; Roman Santillan, College of Staten Island; Marc Schuster, Montgomery County Community College; Carol Singley, Rutgers–Camden; Brenda Siragusa, Corinthian Colleges Inc.; John Staunton, University of North Caroline–Charlotte; Ryan Stryffeler, Ivy Tech Community College of Indiana; Robert Sturr, Kent State University, Stark Campus; James Tanner, University of North Texas; Alisa Thomas, Toccoa Falls College; Nathan Tipton, The University of Memphis; Gary Totten, North Dakota State University; Tony Trigilio, Columbia College, Chicago; Pat Tyrer, West Texas A&M University; Becky Villarreal, Austin Community College; Edward Walkiewicz, Oklahoma State University; Jay Watson, University of Mississippi; Karen Weekes, Penn State Abington; Bruce Weiner, St. Lawrence University; Cindy Weinstein, California Institute of Technology; Stephanie Wells, Orange Coast College; Robert West, Mississippi State University; Diane Whitley Bogard, Austin Community College–Eastview Campus; Edlie Wong, Rutgers; and Beth Younger, Drake University.

In addition, we would like to thank the indefatigable staff at Cengage Learning/Wadsworth for their tireless efforts to make these booklets and the upcoming anthology a reality: Michael Rosenberg, Publisher; Michell Phifer, Senior Development Editor, Lianne Ames, Senior Content Project Manager, Megan Garvey, Assistant Editor; Rebekah Matthews, Editorial Assistant, Emily Ryan, Associate Development Project Manager, Mandee Eckersley, Managing Marketing Manager, Stacey Purviance, Marketing Communications Manager, and Cate Barr, Art Director. We would also like to thank Kathy Smith, Project Manager, for her patience and attention to detail.

—Jay Parini, Middlebury College

# Imagining Gender

Gender issues are central to the development of realism as the dominant literary mode of the post–Civil War period. While romanticism often focused on the relationship of some extraordinary individual to nature, realism tends to explore social relationships, especially those between men and women. For many of the American romantics, women were a relatively minor concern: Thoreau could imagine an idealized life in Nature in *Walden* without thinking about women, and Melville could fashion an epic like *Moby-Dick* without giving women characters more than minor roles. Realism, however, is fundamentally different; it is deeply and intrinsically concerned with the lives of women in real social settings. It rejects the transcendental concern with the Emersonian Oversoul and all other romantic fantasies about some abstract union with nature in favor of a scrutiny of the daily lives of men and women in specific social settings, with detailed attention to both the choices individuals make and the consequences of those choices.

Realism insists that the lives of common men and women matter and that literature should be concerned with the nuances of human interaction and the realities of social relationships. That means a greater commitment to rendering the details of normal life: it means attempting to reproduce the way people actually speak, dress, and act in a variety of social settings. Realism has proven to be the most congenial form for most of our major American women writers, partly because its focus on social relationships, on choices and consequences, on the social and psychological development of individuals, and on the specific details of daily life have enabled these writers to articulate the aspirations and frustrations of American women. In fact, American realism is largely the invention of women writers. Although scholars have found many antebellum sources for the development of realism as a literary mode, it seems increasingly clear that much of the credit belongs to a group of women writers who began to chart the domestic life of women in the 1860s, perhaps most notably Harriet Beecher Stowe, Rose Terry Cooke, Rebecca Harding Davis, and Elizabeth Stuart Phelps Ward. These writers showed that the kitchen could provide as significant a dramatic setting as a wilderness scene and that the comedies and tragedies of domestic life in the United States could inspire laughter or sympathy from readers. They made the lives of women into subjects central to the development of American fiction in the late nineteenth and early twentieth centuries.

The stories that make up this thematic section reflect the variety of ways in which gender emerged as a crucial subject during the formative years of realism in the works of both men and women. Rebecca Harding Davis writes about the trials of an aspiring female author. Harriet Prescott Spofford deals with a woman in a

Depictions of domestic life and gender roles became an important subject of both literature and art in the late nineteenth century as in this photograph (c. 1900) by Jeanette Bernard.

*Courtesy The Art Archive/ Culver Pictures*

madhouse. Frank Stockton tells of a man whose life depends upon drawing the right conclusion about the woman who loves him. Marietta Holley provides a comic assault on the gender assumptions of her time. Thomas Bailey Aldrich explores the ways in which a woman becomes the subject of the male imagination and the object of male fantasies. Constance Fenimore Woolson focuses on a woman who enters a male world and transforms it, at least for a time. These works vary widely in style, setting, and mood, thus demonstrating the many ways in which gender roles shaped the social and psychological underpinnings of the popular fiction of the time. Some of the stories deal with the frustrations of women as they seek to cope with the limitations imposed upon them by society or by marriage. Others focus primarily on the way in which the ideology of gender—the ideas that men and women hold about the proper roles of each sex—shape the possibilities open to individuals in a society that claims to value the democratic ideals of liberty, equality, and opportunity. Some of the most interesting recent feminist criticism focuses on the idea of the "male gaze," on the way men look at women without really seeing complete individuals, on the way men can turn women into imaginative constructs that actually reflect male desires and fantasies. Many of the works of fiction that established realism as a powerful mode focus on the ways men imagine women in terms of their own psychic needs and desires, instead of honestly confronting women as real human beings with their own individual needs and desires. In some of these works, women exist in the male mind primarily as objects, as fantasies that sometimes seem to tell us more about male desire than female hope. In others, women struggle to achieve a sense of meaningful identity in spite of a world that seems to impose arbitrary limits and obstacles. The ways in which men conceive of women play crucial roles in all the stories represented here, but these stories are also concerned with the ways in which women define themselves and their relationships with both men and with other women. The texts that follow provide a variety of responses to gender issues, some comic and some tragic, but they share a deep concern with the ways in which men and women imagine gender and thus help to create the reality that shapes human relationships.

## Rebecca Harding Davis 1831–1910

Remembered today mostly for a single long story, "Life in the Iron Mills," Rebecca Harding Davis was a prolific writer whose best work vividly portrayed the misery of the poor and assailed social injustice. It was the grim but impassioned treatment of unjust suffering in "Life in the Iron Mills" that first drew attention to the young author when it appeared in the *Atlantic Monthly* in 1861 and again led to renewed interest in her work when Tillie Olsen reprinted the tale in a Feminist Press edition in 1972. As Jean Pfaelzer's *A Rebecca Harding Davis Reader* (1995) demonstrates, Davis produced a great deal of other fiction that merits attention. No other woman writer portrayed the horrors of the Civil War more effectively than Davis did in the 1862 stories: "John Lamar," "David Gaunt," and "Blind Tom." Although she wrote an enormous number of stories, many of which appeared in magazines anonymously, she published only one collection of short fiction, *Silhouettes of American Life* (1892). She also produced several novels, the most important of which are *Margaret Howth* (1862), which again engages the grim reality of industrial life; *Waiting for the Verdict* (1867), a powerful attack on racial injustice; and *A Law Unto Herself* (1878), which assails the legal basis of sexism. Like other writers of her time, Davis also wrote many works for children and numerous essays on a wide range of subjects. One of her best works, "A Faded Leaf of History," engages the meaning of American frontier history with a remarkable blend of the historical essay and fictional musing. Davis did little to foster her own literary reputation, and by the time of her death was known primarily as the mother of Richard Harding Davis, one of the most popular writers of the first decades of the twentieth century. Today, the literary achievements of both mother and son remain unjustly neglected, but it seems clear that Rebecca Harding Davis will at least have some place in the literary canon as a pioneer of social realism.

It is possible to select some of Davis's writings out of context and conclude that she was actually a remarkably conservative figure who felt that the primary responsibility of women entailed the responsibilities of motherhood and the home. A fuller review of her considerable output reveals a woman who thought deeply about the social and moral issues of her time and challenged simple complacency in almost everything she wrote. She could be excessively didactic and sentimental, but her strongest work is endowed with genuine power. The story, "Marcia," reprinted below, confronts the dilemma of the woman artist in a world dominated by men. "Marcia," which originally appeared in *Harper's* in 1876, deserves recognition as a carefully wrought and complex treatment of the plight of the woman who aspires to the creation of literature but ultimately finds herself limited to a domestic life devoid of artistic creativity. The story thus draws attention to what will be one of the central themes of later American women writers, including Kate Chopin and Willa Cather.

**Further Reading** Sharon M. Harris, *Rebecca Harding Davis and American Realism* (1991); Jean Pfaelzer, *Parlor Radical: Rebecca Harding Davis and the Origins of American Social Realism* (1997).

# Marcia

ONE winter morning a few years ago the mail brought me a roll of MS. (with one stamp too many, as if to bribe the post to care for so precious a thing) and a letter. Every publisher, editor, or even the obscurest of writers receives such packages so often as to know them at a glance. Half a dozen poems or a story—a blur of sunsets, duchesses, violets, bad French, and worse English; not a solid grain of common-sense, not a hint of reality or even of possibility, in the whole of it. The letter—truth in every word: formal, hard, practical, and the meaning of it a woman's cry for bread for her hungry children.

Each woman who writes such a letter fancies that she is the first, that its pathos will move hard-hearted editors, and that the extent of her need will supply the lack of wit, wisdom, or even grammar in her verses or story. Such appeals pour in literally by the thousand every year to every publishing office. The sickly daughter of a poor family; the wife of a drunken husband; a widow; children that must be fed and clothed. What is the critic's honest opinion of her work? how much will it bring in dollars and cents? etc., etc.

I did not open the letter that day. When we reach middle age we have learned, through rough experiences, how many tragedies there are in our street or under our own roof which will be none the better for our handling, and are apt, selfishly, to try to escape the hearing of them.

This letter, however, when I opened it next morning, proved to be not of a trag-ical sort. The writer was "not dependent on her pen for support"; she "had vowed herself to literature"; she was "resolved to assist in the Progress of humanity." Scarcely had I laid down the letter when I was told that she waited below to see me. The card she sent up was a bit of the fly-leaf of a book, cut oblong with scissors, and the name—Miss Barr—written in imitation of engraving. Her back was toward me when I came down, and I had time to read the same sham stylishness written all over her thin little person. The sleazy black silk was looped in the prevailing fashion, a sweeping white plume drooped from the cheap hat, and on her hands were washed cotton gloves.

Instead of the wizened features of the "dead beat" which I expected, she turned on me a child's face: an ugly face, I believe other women called it, but one of the most innocent and honest in the world. Her brown eyes met mine eagerly, full of a joyous good-fellowship for everything and everybody alive. She poured out her story, too, in a light-hearted way, and in the lowest, friendliest of voices. To see the girl was to be her ally. "People will do anything for me—but publish my manu-scripts," she said.

She came from Mississippi; had been the only white child on a poor plantation on the banks of the Yazoo. "I have only had such teaching as my mother could give: she had but two years with a governess. We had no books nor newspapers, except an occasional copy of a magazine sent to us by friends in the North." Her mother was the one central figure in the world to her then. In our after-intercourse she talked of her continually. "She is a little woman—less than I; but she has one of the finest minds in the world," she would cry. "The sight of anything beautiful or the sound of music sways her as the wind does a reed. But she never was twenty miles from the plantation; she has read nothing, knows nothing. My father thinks women are like mares—only useful to bring forth children. My mother's children all died in babyhood but me. There she has lived all her life, with the swamp on one side and the forest of live-oak on the other: nothing to do, nothing to think of. Oh, it was frightful! With a mind like hers, any woman would go mad, with that eternal forest and swamp, and the graves of her dead babies just in sight! She rubbed snuff a good deal to quiet herself, but of late years she has taken opium."

"And you?"

"I left her. I hoped to do something for us both. My mind is not of as high order as hers, but it is very different from that of most women. I shall succeed some day," in the most matter-of-fact tones. "As soon as I knew that I was a poet I determined to come to Philadelphia and go straight to real publishers and real editors. In my country nobody had ever seen a man who had written a book. Ever since I came here I find how hard it is to find out anything about the business of authorship. Medicine, or law, or black-smithing—everybody knows the workings of those trades, but people with pens in their hands keep the secret of their craft like Freemasons," laughing.

"You came alone?"

"Quite alone. I hired a little room over a baker's shop in Pine Street. They are a very decent couple, the baker and his wife. I board myself, and send out my manuscripts. They always come back to me."

"Where do you send them?"

"Oh, everywhere. I can show you printed forms of rejection from every magazine and literary newspaper in the country," opening and shutting again a black satchel on her lap. "I have written three novels, and sent them to the——s' and——s'. They sent them back as unavailable. But they never read them. I trick them this a-way: I put a loose blue thread between the third and fourth pages of the manuscript, and it is always there when it comes back." Her voice broke a little, but she winked her brown eyes and laughed bravely.

"How long have you been here?"

"Three years."

"Impossible! You are but a child."

"I am twenty. I had an article published once in a Sunday paper," producing a slip about two inches long.

Three years, and only that little grain of success! She had supported herself meanwhile, as I learned afterward, by sewing men's socks for a firm in Germantown.

"You are ready to give up now?"

"No; not if it were ten years instead of three."

Yet I can swear there was not a drop of New England blood in her little body. One was certain, against all reason, that she would succeed. When even such puny creatures as this take the world by the throat in that fashion, they are sure to conquer it.

Her books and poems must, I think, have seemed unique to any editor. The spelling was atrocious; the errors of grammar in every line beyond remedy. The lowest pupil in our public schools would have detected her ignorance on the first page. There was, too, in all that she said or wrote an occasional gross indecency, such as a child might show: her life on the plantation explained it. Like Juliet she spoke the language of her nurse. But even Shakspeare's nurse and Juliet would not be allowed nowadays to chatter at will in the pages of a family magazine.

But in all her ignorance, mistakes, and weaknesses there was no trace of imitation. She plagiarized nobody. There was none of the usual talk of countesses, heather, larks, or emotions of which she knew nothing. She painted over and over again her own home on the Yazoo: the hot still sunshine, the silence of noon, the swamp, the slimy living things in the stagnant ponds, the semi-tropical forest, the house and negro quarters, with all their dirt and dreary monotony. It was a picture which remained in the mind strong and vivid as one of Gêrome's deserts or Hardy's moors.[1]

There could be but one kind of advice to give her—to put away pen and ink, and for three years at least devote herself to hard study. She would, of course, have none of such counsel. The popular belief in the wings of genius, which can carry it over hard work and all such obstacles as ignorance of grammar or even the spelling-book, found in her a marked example. Work was for commonplace talent, not for those whose veins were full of the divine ichor.[2]

Meanwhile she went on sewing socks, and sending off her great yellow envelopes, with stamps to bring them back.

"Stamps and paper count up so fast!" she said, with a laugh, into which had grown a pitiful quaver. She would take not a penny of aid. "I shall not starve. When the time has come for me to know that I have failed, I can go back to my own country and live like the other women there."

Meanwhile her case very nearly reached starvation. I remember few things more pathetic than the damp, forlorn little figure in a shabby water-proof, black satchel in hand, which used to come to our door through the snows and drenching rains that winter. Her shoes were broken, and her hands shrivelled blue with cold. But a plated gilt chain or a scarlet ribbon used to flaunt somewhere over the meagre, scant poverty. Sometimes she brought news with her. She had work given her—to collect a column of jokes for a Sunday paper, by which she made three dollars a week. But she lost it from trying to insert her own matter, which could not well be reckoned as funny sayings. One day she came flushed with excitement. Somebody had taken her through the Academy of Design and a private gallery of engravings then on exhibition. She had a keen, just eye for form and color, and the feeling of a true artist for both.

"That is what I could have done," she said, after keeping silence a long while. "But what chance had I? I never even saw a picture at home, except those which were cut out of illustrated papers. There seemed to be no way for me but to write."

It was suggested to her that she might find the other way even now. Painting, designing, wood-engraving, were expressions for a woman's mind, even though, like her own, it was "one of the finest in the world."

---

[1] **Gêrome's deserts or Hardy's moors:** The landscapes created by the French painter, Jean-Léon Gérôme (1824–1904), and the English novelist, Thomas Hardy (1840–1928).
[2] **ichor:** The fluid that runs in the veins of the gods in Greek mythology.

She did not smile. "It is too late," she said. "I will go on as I have begun. But it is a pity my mother and I had not known of such things."

After that her light-hearted courage seemed to give way. She persevered, but it was with dogged, indomitable resolution, and little hope.

One day in the spring I was summoned to see a visitor on business. I found a tall, lank young man stalking up and down the room, the most noticeable point about him the shock of red hair and whisker falling over his neck and greasy coat collar. The face was that of an ignorant, small-minded man. But it was candid and not sensual.

He came straight toward me. "Is Marcia Barr here?"

"No; she has been gone for an hour."

He damned his luck in a white heat of rage, which must, I thought, have required some time to kindle. Indeed, I found he had been pacing up and down the street half the morning, having seen her come in. She had gone out by a side door.

"I caught a glimpse of her half a mile off. I have come to Philadelphia three times this year to find her. Good God! how rank poor she is! Where does she live?"

I could not tell him, as Marcia had long ago left the baker's, and changed her quarters every month.

"And I reckon I'll have to wait until she comes hyah again. Tell her it's Zack Biron,[3] the overseer's son, on—on business."

He was not long in unveiling his business, which any woman would soon have guessed. He had come to bring Marcia home and marry her. He had always "wanted her," and the old colonel, her father, had promised he should marry her provided he could bring her back from her mad flight. The colonel was dead, and he was now "runnin' the plantation for ole madam. She's no better than a walkin' corpse, with that damned drug she chews. She can't keep still now: walks, walks incessant about the place, with her eyes set an' the skin clingin' to her bones. I couldn't 'a borne it, I ashuah you, but for the sake of findin' Marcia."

Two months passed, in which he haunted the house. But Marcia did not come. She had begun to frequent newspaper offices, and occasionally was given a trifling bit of work by the managers of the reporting corps—a description of the dresses at a Männerchor ball to write, or a puff of some coming play, etc. She came at last to tell me of what she had done.

"It is miserable work. I would rather sew the heels of stockings; but the stocking looms have stopped, and I must live a little longer, at any rate. I think I have something to say, if people only would hear it."

I told her of Biron and his chase for her.

"I saw him outside the window the last time I was here. That was the reason I went out by the side street. I knew he was looking for me. You will not tell him I have been here?"

---

[3] **Biron:** The name ironically highlights his contrasts to the great English romantic poet, Lord Byron, who was renowned for both his poetry and his extravagant life; Byron was once called "mad, bad, and dangerous to know."

"But, Marcia, the man seems honest and kindly—"

"If he found me," in the same quiet tone, "he would marry me and take me back to the plantation."

"And you are not ready to give up?"

"No, I will not give up. I shall get into the right groove at last," with the infectious little laugh which nobody could resist.

The water-proof cloak was worn down quite into the cotton by this time, and the straw hat had been darned around the ragged edge. But there was a cheap red rose in it. Her cheek-bones showed high, and her eyes shone out of black hollows.

"No, I have no cough, and I don't need medicine," she said, irritably, when questioned. "I have had plenty of offers of help. But I'd rather steal than take alms." She rose hastily and buttoned her cloak.

"This man Biron waits only a word to come to you. He is faithful as a dog."

She nodded carelessly. Biron, or a return to her old home, held no part in her world, it was plain to see.

I was out of the city for several months. A few weeks after my return I saw in the evening paper one day, in the usual list of crimes and casualties, an item headed *"Pitiable Case.*—A young woman named Burr was arrested yesterday on charge of theft, and taken to the Central Station. About eleven o'clock the other women in the cell where she was confined perceiving that she lay on a bench breathing in a stertorous manner, summoned Lieutenant Pardy, who found life to be almost extinct. A physician was called, who discovered that the woman had swallowed some poisonous drug. With her first breath of returning consciousness she protested her innocence of the charge. She appears to have been in an extreme state of want. But little hope is entertained of her recovery. Miss Burr is favorably known, we believe, as a writer of some ability for the daily press."

In spite of the difference of name, it must be Marcia.

When we reached the Central Station we were told that her discharge was already procured. She had friends who knew what wires to work. In the outer room were half a dozen young men, reporters, a foreman of a printing-room, and one or two women, dramatic or musical critics. There is as eager an *esprit de corps* among that class of journalists as among actors. They were all talking loudly, and zealous in defence of "Little Marty," as they called her, whom they declared to be "a dunce so far as head went, but pure and guileless as a child."

"I knew she was devilishly hard up," said one, "but never suspected she was starving. She would not borrow a dollar, she had that pride in her."

Marcia was still in the cell, lying on an iron stretcher. The Mississippian, Biron, was with her, kneeling on the floor in his shirt sleeves, chafing her hand. He had taken off his coat to wrap about her.

"I've a good Quaker nurse and a room ready for her at the Continental the minute she can be moved," he whispered. "Look a-here!" turning down the poor bit of lace and red ribbon at her throat, his big hairy hand shaking. "Them bones is a'most through the skin! The doctor says it's hunger—hunger! And *I* was eatin' three solid meals a day—like a beast!"

Hunger had almost done its work. There was but a feeble flicker of life left in the emaciated little body; not enough to know or speak to us when at last she opened her dull eyes.

"None o' them folks need consarn themselves any furder about her," said Biron savagely. "She'll come home to her own now, thank God, and be done with rubbishy book-makers. Mrs. Biron will live like a lady."

Two or three weeks later, the most splendid of hired phaetons stopped at my door, and Mr. and Mrs. Biron sent up their cards. Mr. Biron was glowing with happiness. It asserted itself offensively somehow in the very jingling of his watch chain and tie of his cravat.

"We return immediately to the plantation," he said, grandiloquently. "I reckon largely on the effect of her native air in restorin' Mrs. Biron to health."

Marcia was magnificent in silk and plumes, the costliest that her owner's money could buy. Her little face was pale, however, and she looked nobody in the eye.

"We leave for the South to-morrow," she said, calmly, "and I shall not return to Philadelphia. I have no wish to return."

"Shall I send you books or papers, Marcia?"

"No, I thank you; nothing."

When, they rose to go, her husband said, "Mrs. Biron has some—rubbish she wishes to leave with you. Hyah!" calling out of the window. "You nigger, bring that thah bag!"

It was the old black satchel. Marcia took it in her white-gloved hands, half opened it, shut it quickly, came up closer.

"These are my manuscripts," she said. "Will you burn them for me? All; do not leave a line, a word. I could not do it."

I took the satchel, and they departed. Mr. Biron was vehement in his protestations of friendship and invitations to visit the plantation.

But Marcia did not say a word, even of farewell.

—1876

# Frank Stockton 1834–1902

Among the most famous and most popular writers of his time, Frank Stockton won a huge readership with his facetious style and clever wit. He began his literary career as a writer for children and served as an assistant editor of *St Nicholas* (1873–1881), the premier publication for children in the United States during the nineteenth century. The nonsense stories he wrote for children led him ultimately to a richer understanding of the possibilities inherent in the fairy tale and the fanciful fable. Although he produced several collections of his work for juveniles, the imaginative possibilities of the fable are best realized in the pieces collected in 1887 in *The Bee Man of Orn and Other Fanciful Tales* (1887), particularly the title story and "The Griffin and the Minor Canon." Stockton turned to writing for adults and achieved a great deal of success with both his comic novels and ingenious stories. His most famous sustained works were the series of books that began with *Rudder Grange* in 1879 and featured a newlywed couple moving into a houseboat with their remarkable maid, Pomona, but his best novels are probably *The Casting Away of Mrs. Lecks and Mrs. Aleshine* (1886) and its sequel, *The Dusantes* (1888), which focus on the comic misadventures and triumphs of two older women. Stockton merits more attention in the history of literary comedy in the United States for his mastery of a humor that is always humane and often ingenious.

Stockton was also a noted short story writer who produced at least one tale that his own time was certain would remain a perennial classic: "The Lady or the Tiger?" (1882). Unfortunately, this story has been almost completely excluded from college reading lists for decades. Its inclusion in the thematic section on "Gender Issues" is designed to emphasize the relevance of Stockton's work for our time. Although it lacks the broader comic vision that marks most of his strongest fiction, "The Lady or the Tiger?" represents Stockton's ability to use popular fiction to raise important questions about the formation of identity and the role of social relationships. Like many of the other stories in this thematic section (and throughout much of American realism), it is deeply concerned with the construction of male and female identity and with the ways in which men imagine women.

**Further Reading** Henry L Golemba, *Frank R. Stockton* (1981); Martin Ignatius Joseph Griffin, *Frank R. Stockton: A Critical Biography* (1939).

# The Lady or the Tiger?

In the very olden time, there lived a semi-barbaric king, whose ideas, though somewhat polished and sharpened by the progressiveness of distant Latin neighbors, were still large, florid, and untrammelled, as became the half of him which was barbaric. He was a man of exuberant fancy, and, withal, of an authority so irresistible that, at his will, he turned his varied fancies into facts. He was greatly given to self-communing, and when he and himself agreed upon anything, the thing was done. When every member of his domestic and political systems moved smoothly in its appointed course, his nature was bland and genial; but whenever there was a little hitch, and some of his orbs got out of their orbits, he was blander and more genial still, for nothing pleased him so much as to make the crooked straight, and crush down uneven places.

Among the borrowed notions by which his barbarism had become semified[1] was that of the public arena, in which, by exhibitions of manly and beastly valor, the minds of his subjects were refined and cultured.

But even here the exuberant and barbaric fancy asserted itself. The arena of the king was built, not to give the people an opportunity of hearing the rhapsodies of

---

[1] **semified:** Reduced to half.

dying gladiators, nor to enable them to view the inevitable conclusion of a conflict between religious opinions and hungry jaws, but for purposes far better adapted to widen and develop the mental energies of the people. This vast amphitheatre, with its encircling galleries, its mysterious vaults, and its unseen passages, was an agent of poetic justice, in which crime was punished, or virtue rewarded, by the decrees of an impartial and incorruptible chance.

When a subject was accused of a crime of sufficient importance to interest the king, public notice was given that on an appointed day the fate of the accused person would be decided in the king's arena—a structure which well deserved its name; for, although its form and plan were borrowed from afar, its purpose emanated solely from the brain of this man, who, every barleycorn a king, knew no tradition to which he owed more allegiance than pleased his fancy, and who ingrafted on every adopted form of human thought and action the rich growth of his barbaric idealism.

When all the people had assembled in the galleries, and the king, surrounded by his court, sat high up on his throne of royal state on one side of the arena, he gave a signal, a door beneath him opened, and the accused subject stepped out into the amphitheatre. Directly opposite him, on the other side of the enclosed space, were two doors, exactly alike and side by side. It was the duty and the privilege of the person on trial to walk directly to these doors and open one of them. He could open either door he pleased. He was subject to no guidance or influence but that of the aforementioned impartial and incorruptible chance. If he opened the one, there came out of it a hungry tiger, the fiercest and most cruel that could be procured, which immediately sprang upon him, and tore him to pieces, as a punishment for his guilt. The moment that the case of the criminal was thus decided, doleful iron bells were clanged, great wails went up from the hired mourners posted on the outer rim of the arena, and the vast audience, with bowed heads and downcast hearts, wended slowly their homeward way, mourning greatly that one so young and fair, or so old and respected, should have merited so dire a fate.

But if the accused person opened the other door, there came forth from it a lady, the most suitable to his years and station that his Majesty could select among his fair subjects; and to this lady he was immediately married, as a reward of his innocence. It mattered not that he might already possess a wife and family, or that his affections might be engaged upon an object of his own selection. The king allowed no such subordinate arrangements to interfere with his great scheme of retribution and reward. The exercises, as in the other instance, took place immediately, and in the arena. Another door opened beneath the king, and a priest, followed by a band of choristers, and dancing maidens blowing joyous airs on golden horns and treading an epithalamic measure, advanced to where the pair stood side by side, and the wedding was promptly and cheerily solemnized. Then the gay brass bells rang forth their merry peals, the people shouted glad hurrahs, and the innocent man, preceded by children strewing flowers on his path, led his bride to his home.

Albert Herter's illustration of the male protagonist awaiting his fate in "The Lady or the Tiger?" appeared in the 1900 collected edition of Stockton's work.

*From The Novels and Stories of Frank R. Stockton. Stories 1 (New York: Charles Scribner's Sons)*

This was the king's semibarbaric method of administering justice. Its perfect fairness is obvious. The criminal could not know out of which door would come the lady. He opened either he pleased, without having the slightest idea whether, in the next instant, he was to be devoured or married. On some occasions the tiger came out of one door, and on some out of the other. The decisions of this tribunal were not only fair—they were positively determinate. The accused person was instantly punished if he found himself guilty, and if innocent he was rewarded on the spot, whether he liked it or not. There was no escape from the judgments of the king's arena.

The institution was a very popular one. When the people gathered together on one of the great trial days, they never knew whether they were to witness a bloody slaughter or a hilarious wedding. This element of uncertainty lent an interest to the occasion which it could not otherwise have attained. Thus the masses were entertained and pleased, and the thinking part of the community could bring no charge of unfairness against this plan; for did not the accused person have the whole matter in his own hands?

This semi-barbaric king had a daughter as blooming as his most florid fancies, and with a soul as fervent and imperious as his own. As is usual in such cases, she was the apple of his eye, and was loved by him above all humanity. Among his courtiers was a young man of that fineness of blood and lowness of station common to the conventional heroes of romance who love royal maidens. This royal maiden was well satisfied with her lover, for he was handsome and brave to a degree unsurpassed in all this kingdom, and she loved him with an ardor that had enough of barbarism in it to make it exceedingly warm and strong. This love affair moved on happily for many months, until, one day, the king happened to discover its existence. He did not hesitate nor waver in regard to his duty in the premises. The youth was immediately cast into prison, and a day was appointed for his trial in the king's arena. This, of course, was an especially important occasion, and his Majesty, as well as all the people, was greatly interested in the workings and development of this trial. Never before had such a case occurred—never before had a subject dared to love the daughter of a king. In after years such things became commonplace enough, but then they were, in no slight degree, novel and startling.

The tiger cages of the kingdom were searched for the most savage and relentless beasts, from which the fiercest monster might be selected for the arena, and the ranks of maiden youth and beauty throughout the land were carefully surveyed by competent judges, in order that the young man might have a fitting bride in case fate did not determine for him a different destiny. Of course, everybody knew that the deed with which the accused was charged had been done. He had loved the princess, and neither he, she, nor any one else thought of denying the fact. But the king would not think of allowing any fact of this kind to interfere with the workings of the tribunal, in which he took such great delight and satisfaction. No matter how the affair turned out, the youth would be disposed of, and the king would take an æsthetic pleasure in watching the course of events which would determine whether or not the young man had done wrong in allowing himself to love the princess.

The appointed day arrived. From far and near the people gathered, and thronged the great galleries of the arena, while crowds, unable to gain admittance, massed themselves against its outside walls. The king and his court were in their places, opposite the twin doors—those fateful portals, so terrible in their similarity!

All was ready. The signal was given. A door beneath the royal party opened, and the lover of the princess walked into the arena. Tall, beautiful, fair, his appearance was greeted with a low hum of admiration and anxiety. Half the audience had not known so grand a youth had lived among them. No wonder the princess loved him! What a terrible thing for him to be there!

As the youth advanced into the arena, he turned, as the custom was, to bow to the king. But he did not think at all of that royal personage; his eyes were fixed upon the princess, who sat to the right of her father. Had it not been for the moiety of barbarism in her nature, it is probable that lady would not have been there. But her intense and fervid soul would not allow her to be absent on an occasion in which she was so terribly interested. From the moment that the decree had gone forth that her lover should decide his fate in the king's arena, she had thought of nothing, night or day, but this great event and the various subjects connected with it. Possessed of more power, influence, and force of character than any one who had ever before been interested in such a case, she had done what no other person had done—she had possessed herself of the secret of the doors. She knew in which of the two rooms behind those doors stood the cage of the tiger, with its open front, and in which waited the lady. Through these thick doors, heavily curtained with skins on the inside, it was impossible that any noise or suggestion should come from within to the person who should approach to raise the latch of one of them. But gold, and the power of a woman's will, had brought the secret to the princess.

Not only did she know in which room stood the lady, ready to emerge, all blushing and radiant, should her door be opened, but she knew who the lady was. It was one of the fairest and loveliest of the damsels of the court who had been selected as the reward of the accused youth, should he be proved innocent of the crime of aspiring to one so far above him; and the princess hated her. Often had she seen, or imagined that she had seen, this fair creature throwing glances of admiration upon the person of her lover, and sometimes she thought these glances were perceived and even returned. Now and then she had seen them talking together. It was but for a moment or two, but much can be said in a brief space. It may have been on most unimportant topics, but how could she know that? The girl was lovely, but she had dared to raise her eyes to the loved one of the princess, and, with all the intensity of the savage blood transmitted to her through long lines of wholly barbaric ancestors, she hated the woman who blushed and trembled behind that silent door.

When her lover turned and looked at her, and his eye met hers as she sat there paler and whiter than any one in the vast ocean of anxious faces about her, he saw, by that power of quick perception which is given to those whose souls are one, that she knew behind which door crouched the tiger, and behind which stood the lady. He had expected her to know it. He understood her nature, and his soul was assured that she would never rest until she had made plain to herself this thing, hidden to all other lookers-on, even to the king. The only hope for the youth in which there was any element of certainty was based upon the success of the princess in discovering this mystery, and the moment he looked upon her, he saw she had succeeded.

Then it was that his quick and anxious glance asked the question, "Which?" It was as plain to her as if he shouted it from where he stood. There was not an instant to be lost. The question was asked in a flash; it must be answered in another.

Her right arm lay on the cushioned parapet before her. She raised her hand, and made a slight, quick movement toward the right. No one but her lover saw her. Every eye but his was fired on the man in the arena.

He turned, and with a firm and rapid step he walked across the empty space. Every heart stopped beating, every breath was held, every eye was fixed immovably upon that man. Without the slightest hesitation, he went to the door on the right, and opened it.

Now, the point of the story is this: Did the tiger come out of that door, or did the lady?

The more we reflect upon this question, the harder it is to answer. It involves a study of the human heart which leads us through devious mazes of passion, out of which it is difficult to find our way. Think of it, fair reader, not as if the decision of the question depended upon yourself, but upon that hot-blooded, semi-barbaric princess, her soul at a white heat beneath the combined fires of despair and jealousy. She had lost him, but who should have him?

How often, in her waking hours and in her dreams, had she started in wild horror and covered her face with her hands as she thought of her lover opening the door on the other side of which waited the cruel fangs of the tiger!

But how much oftener had she seen him at the other door! How in her grievous reveries had she gnashed her teeth and torn her hair when she saw his start of rapturous delight as he opened the door of the lady! How her soul had burned in agony when she had seen him rush to meet that woman, with her flushing cheek and sparkling eye of triumph; when she had seen him lead her forth, his whole frame kindled with the joy of recovered life; when she had heard the glad shouts from the multitude, and the wild ringing of the happy bells; when she had seen the priest, with his joyous followers, advance to the couple, and make them man and wife before her very eyes; and when she had seen them walk away together upon their path of flowers, followed by the tremendous shouts of the hilarious multitude, in which her one despairing shriek was lost and drowned!

Would it not be better for him to die at once, and go to wait for her in the blessed regions of semi-barbaric futurity?

And yet, that awful tiger, those shrieks, that blood!

Her decision had been indicated in an instant, but it had been made after days and nights of anguished deliberation. She had known she would be asked, she had decided what she would answer, and, without the slightest hesitation, she had moved her hand to the right.

The question of her decision is one not to be lightly considered, and it is not for me to presume to set up myself as the one person able to answer it. So I leave it with all of you: Which came out of the opened door—the lady or the tiger?

—1882

# Harriet Prescott Spofford  1835–1921

Harriet Prescott Spofford earned an enviable reputation as a promising young writer of fiction with the publication of three remarkable tales in the *Atlantic Monthly*: "In the Cellar" (1859), "Circumstance" (1860), and "The Amber Gods" (1860). In their lavish use of symbolism and lush language, their exotic settings and extraordinary characters, these stories represent the final flowering of romantic fiction in New England. Spofford went on to a long career as a writer of fiction, poetry, and essays, but her literary reputation faded away very quickly. Part of the problem was that financial pressures drove her to write too much, too quickly, and she could not sustain the high level of achievement set by her earliest tales in the *Atlantic*. She also had difficulty adapting her romantic inclinations to a marketplace that increasingly demanded realism.

Spofford did her best to comply with the demands of the market and continued to write and publish prolifically, but the hundreds of stories that followed did not draw the critical attention and acclaim of her earliest work. She became known as a "magazinist," a writer who could be relied on for an amusing tale, but not one that need be taken seriously. Nevertheless, there were a few moments in her later career when Spofford managed to combine the imaginative grasp of romantic fiction with the clarity and precision of realism, most notably the work reprinted here, "Her Story" (1872), which should probably be ranked as her finest achievement in fiction. There have been recent signs that Spofford's early work may enter the canon at least in a modest way; most of the major anthologies of American Literature now include "Circumstance," but in several respects, "Her Story" offers a better introduction to this writer. The story concerns an intricate triangle—the nameless narrator who tells her story in a madhouse in hopes that storytelling can lead to liberation; the egotistical husband to whom she sacrifices her identity and her sanity; and the other woman, a demonic figure at first who ultimately becomes another victim of male arrogance and the ironic companion of our narrator. In its treatment of madness, "Her Story" provides a foreshadowing of and intriguing counterpart to Gilman's "The Yellow Wallpaper." In its fully developed characterization and plot, the tale confronts gender issues with imaginative power and genuine insight.

**Further Reading** Alfred Bendixen, Introduction, *The Amber Gods and Other Stories* by Harriet Prescott Spofford (1989), ix–xxxix; Eva Gold and Thomas H. Fick, "A Masterpiece of the 'Educated Eye': Convention, Gaze, and Gender in Spofford's 'Her Story,'" *Studies in Short Fiction* 30.4 (1993): 511–523; Elizabeth K. Halbeisen, *Harriet Prescott Spofford: A Romantic Survival* (1935).

# Her Story

WELLNIGH the worst of it all is the mystery.

If it were true, that accounts for my being here. If it were not true, then the best thing they could do with me was to bring me here. Then, too, if it were true, they would save themselves by hurrying me away; and if it were not true— You see, just as all roads lead to Rome, all roads led me to this Retreat. If it were true, it was enough to craze me; and if it were not true, I was already crazed. And there it is! I can't make out, sometimes, whether I am really beside myself or not; for it seems that whether I was crazed or sane, if it were true, they would naturally put me out of sight and hearing— bury me alive, as they have done, in this Retreat. They? Well, no—he. She stayed at home, I hear. If she had come with us, doubtless I should have found reason enough to say to the physician at once that she was the mad woman, not I—she, who, for the sake of her own brief pleasure, could make a whole after-life of misery for three of us. She— Oh no, don't rise, don't go. I am quite myself, I am perfectly calm. Mad! There was never a drop of crazy blood in the Ridgleys or the Bruces, or any of the generations behind them, and why should it suddenly break out like a smothered fire in me? That is one of the things that puzzle me—why should it come to light all at once in me if it were not true?

Now, I am not going to be incoherent. It was too kind in you to be at such trouble to come and see me in this prison, this grave. I will not cry out once: I will just tell you the story of it all exactly as it was, and you shall judge. If I can, that is—oh, if I can! For sometimes, when I think of it, it seems as if Heaven itself would fail to take my part if I did not lift my own voice. And I cry, and I tear my hair and my flesh, till I know my anguish weighs down their joy, and the little scale that holds that joy flies up under the scorching of the sun, and God sees the festering thing for what it is! Ah, it is not injured reason that cries out in that way: it is a breaking heart!

How cool your hand is, how pleasant your face is, how good it is to see you! Don't be afraid of me: I am as much myself, I tell you, as you are. What an absurdity! Certainly any one who heard me make such a speech would think I was insane and without benefit of clergy. To ask you not to be afraid of me because I am myself. Isn't it what they call a vicious circle? And then to cap the climax by adding that I am as much myself as you are myself! But no matter—you know better. Did you say it was ten years? Yes, I knew it was as much as that—oh, it seems a hundred years! But we hardly show it: your hair is still the same as when we were at school; and mine— Look at this lock—I cannot understand why it is only sprinkled here and there: it ought to be white as the driven snow. My babies are almost grown women, Elizabeth. How could he do without me all this time? Hush now! I am not going to be disturbed at all; only that color of your hair puts me so in mind of his: perhaps there was just one trifle more of gold in his. Do you remember that lock that used to fall over his forehead and which he always tossed back so impatiently. I used to think that the golden Apollo of Rhodes had just such massive, splendid locks of hair as that; but I never told him; I never had the face to praise him; she had. She could exclaim how like ivory the forehead was—that great wide forehead—how that keen aquiline was to be found in the portrait of the Spencer of two hundred years ago. She could tell of the proud lip, of the fire burning in the hazel eye. She knew how, by a silent flattery, as she shrank away and looked up at him, to admire his haughty stature, and make him feel the strength and glory of his manhood and the delicacy of her womanhood.

She was a little thing—a little thing, but wondrous fair. Fair, did I say? No: she was dark as an Egyptian, but such perfect features, such rich and splendid color, such great soft eyes—so soft, so black—so superb a smile; and then such hair! When she let it down, the backward curling ends lay on the ground and she stood on them, or the children lifted them and carried them behind her as pages carry a queen's train. If I had my two hands twisted in that hair! Oh, how I hate that hair! It would make as good a bowstring as ever any Carthaginian woman's made.

Ah, that is atrocious! I am sure you think so. But living all these lonesome years as I have done seems to double back one's sinfulness upon one's self. Because one is sane it does not follow that one is a saint. And when I think of my innocent babies playing with the hair that once I saw him lift and pass across his lips! But I will not think of it!

Well, well! I was a pleasant thing to look at myself once on a time, you know, Elizabeth. He used to tell me so: those were his very words. I was tall and slender, and if my skin was pale it was clear with a pearly clearness, and the lashes of my gray eyes were black as shadows; but now those eyes are only the color of tears.

I never told a syllable about it—I never could. It was so deep down in my heart, that love I had for him: it slept there so dark and still and full, for he was all I had in the world. I was alone, an orphan—if not friendless, yet quite dependent. I see you remember it all. I did not even sit in the pew with my cousin's family,—there were so many to fill it,—but down in one beneath the gallery, you know. And altogether life was a thing to me that hardly seemed worth the living. I went to church one Sunday, I recollect, idly and dreamingly as usual. I did not look off my book till a voice filled my ear—a strange new voice, a deep sweet voice, that invited you and yet commanded you—a voice whose sound divided the core of my heart, and sent thrills that were half joy, half pain, coursing through me. And then I looked up and saw him at the desk. He was reading the first lesson: "Fear not, for I have redeemed thee, I have called thee by thy name: thou art mine." And I saw the bright hair, the bright upturned face, the white surplice, and I said to myself, It is a vision, it is an angel; and I cast down my eyes. But the voice went on, and when I looked again he was still there. Then I bethought me that it must be the one who was coming to take the place of our superannuated rector—the last of a fine line, they had been saying the day before, who, instead of finding his pleasure otherwise, had taken all his wealth and prestige into the Church.

Why will a trifle melt you so—a strain of music, a color in the sky, a perfume? Have you never leaned from the window at evening, and had the scent of a flower float by and fill you with as keen a sorrow as if it had been disaster touching you? Long ago, I mean—we never lean from any windows here. I don't know how, but it was in that same invisible way that this voice melted me; and when I heard it saying, "Behold, I will do a new thing; now it shall spring forth; shall ye not know it? I will even make a way in the wilderness, and rivers in the desert," I was fairly crying. Oh, nervous tears, I dare say. The doctor here would tell you so, at any rate. And that is what I complain of here: they give a physiological reason for every emotion—they could give you a chemical formula for your very soul, I have no doubt. Well, perhaps they were nervous tears, for certainly there was nothing to cry for, and the mood went as suddenly as it came—changed to a sort of exaltation, I suppose—and when they sang the psalm, and he had swept in, in his black gown, and had mounted the pulpit stairs, and was resting that fair head on the big Bible in his silent prayer, I too was singing—singing like one possessed:

"Then, to thy courts when I repair,
    My soul shall rise on joyful wing,
The wonders of thy love declare,
    And join the strain which angels sing."

And as he rose I saw him searching for the voice unconsciously, and our eyes met. Oh, it was a fresh young voice, let it be mine or whose. I can hear it now as if it were someone else singing. Ah, ah, it has been silent so many years! Does it make you smile to hear me pity myself? It is not myself I am pitying: it is that fresh young girl that loved so. But it used to rejoice me to think that I loved him before I laid eyes on him.

He came to my cousin's in the week—not to see Sylvia or to see Laura: he talked of church-music with my cousin, and then crossed the room and sat down by me. I remember how I grew cold and trembled—how glad, how shy I was; and then he had me sing; and at first Sylvia sang with us, but by and by we sang alone—I sang alone. He brought me yellow old church music, written in quaint characters: he said those characters, those old square breves, were a text guarding secrets of enchantment as much as the text of Merlin's book did; and so we used to find it. Once he brought a copy of an old Roman hymn, written only in the Roman letters: he said it was a hymn which the ancients sang to Maia, the mother-earth, and which the Church fathers adopted, singing it stealthily in the hidden places of the Catacombs; and together we translated it into tones. A rude but majestic thing it was.

And once— The sunshine was falling all about us in the bright lonely room, and the shadows of the rose leaves at the window were dancing over us. I had been singing a Gloria while he walked up and down the room, and he came up behind me: he stooped and kissed me on the mouth. And after that there was no more singing, for, lovely as the singing was, the love was lovelier yet. Why do I complain of such a hell as this is now? I had my heaven once—oh, I had my heaven once! And as for the other, perhaps I deserve it all, for I saw God only through him: it was he that waked me to worship. I had no faith but Spencer's faith; if he had been a heathen, I should have been the same, and creeds and systems might have perished for me had he only been spared from the wreck. And he had loved me from the first moment that his eyes met mine. "When I looked at you," he said, "singing that simple hymn that first day, I felt as I do when I look at the evening star leaning out of the clear sunset lustre: there is something in your face as pure, as remote, as shining. It will always be there," he said, "though you should live a hundred years." He little knew, he little knew!

But he loved me then—oh yes, I never doubted that. There were no happier lovers trod the earth. We took our pleasure as lovers do: we walked in the fields; we sat on the river's side; together we visited the poor and sick; he read me the passages he liked best in his writing from week to week; he brought me the verse from which he meant to preach, and up in the organ-loft I improvised to him the thoughts that it inspired in me. I did that timidly indeed: I could not think my thoughts were worth his hearing till I forgot myself, and only thought of him and the glory I would have revealed to him, and then the great clustering chords and the full music of the diapason swept out beneath my hands—swept along the aisles and swelled up the raftered roof as if they would find the stars, and sunset and twilight stole around us there as we sat still in the succeeding silence. I was happy: I was humble too. I wondered why I had been chosen for such a blest and sacred lot. It was so blessed to be allowed to minister one delight to him. I had a little print of the angel of the Lord appearing to Mary with the lily of annunciation in his hand, and I thought—I dare not tell you what I thought. I made an idol of my piece of clay.

When the leaves had turned we were married, and he took me home. Ah, what a happy home it was! Luxury and beauty filled it. When I first went into it and left the chill October night without, fires blazed upon the hearths; flowers bloomed in every room; a marble Eros held a light up, searching for his Psyche. "*Our* love has found its soul," said he. He led me to the music-room—a temple in itself, for its rounded ceiling towered to the height of the house. There were golden organ-pipes and banks of keys fit for St. Cecilia's[1] use; there were all the delightful outlines of violin and piccolo and harp and horn for any who would use them; there was a pianoforte near the door for me—one such as I had never touched before; and there were cases on all sides filled with the rarest musical works. The floor was bare and

---

[1] **St. Cecilia:** Patron saint of musicians; she is sometimes credited with inventing the organ.

inlaid; the windows were latticed in stained glass, so that no common light of day ever filtered through, but light bluer than the sky, gold as the dawn, purple as the night; and then there were vast embowering chairs, in any of which he could hide himself away while I made my incantation, as he sometimes called it, of the great spirits of song. As I tried the piano that night he tuned the old Amati[2] which he himself now and then played upon, and together we improvised our own epithalamium. It was the violin that took the strong assuring part with strains of piercing sweetness, and the music of the piano flowed along in a soft cantabile of undersong. It seemed to me as if his part was like the flight of some white and strong-winged bird above a sunny brook.

But he had hardly created this place for the love of me alone. He adored music as a regenerator; he meant to use it so among his people: here were to be pursued those labors which should work miracles when produced in the open church. For he was building a church with the half of his fortune—a church full of restoration of the old and creation of the new: the walls within were to be a frosty tracery of vines running to break into the gigantic passion-flower that formed the rose-window; the lectern a golden globe upon a tripod, clasped by a silver dove holding on outstretched wings the book.

I have feared, since I have been here, that Spencer's piety was less piety than partisanship: I have doubted if faith were so much alive in him as the love of a great perfect system, and the pride in it I know he always felt. But I never thought about it then: I believed in him as I would have believed in an apostle. So stone by stone the church went up, and stone by stone our lives followed it—lives of such peace, such bliss! Then fresh hopes came into it—sweet trembling hopes; and by and by our first child was born. And if I had been happy before, what was I then? There are some compensations in this world: such happiness could not come twice, such happiness as there was in that moment when I lay, painless and at peace, with the little cheek nestled beside my own, while he bent above us both, proud and glad and tender. It was a dear little baby—so fair, so bright! and when she could walk she could sing. Her sister sang earlier yet; and what music their two shrill sweet voices made as they sat in their little chairs together at twilight before the fire, their curls glistening and their red shoes glistening, while they sang the evening hymn, Spencer on one side of the hearth and I upon the other! Sometimes we let the dear things sit up for a later hour in the music-room—for many a canticle we tried and practised there that hushed hearts and awed them when the choir gave them on succeeding Sundays—and always afterward I heard them singing in their sleep, just as a bird stirs in his nest and sings his stave in the night. Oh, we were happy then; and it was then she came.

She was the step-child of his uncle, and had a small fortune of her own, and Spencer had been left her guardian; and so she was to live with us—at any rate, for a while. I dreaded her coming. I did not want the intrusion; I did not like the things I

---

[2] **Amati:** The seventeenth-century family renowned for the creation of superb violins; their students included Stradivari and Guarnari.

heard about her; I knew she would be a discord in our harmony. But Spencer, who had only seen her once in her childhood, had been told by some one who travelled in Europe with her that she was delightful and had a rare intelligence. She was one of those women often delightful to men indeed, but whom other women—by virtue of their own kindred instincts, it may be, perhaps by virtue of temptations over-come—see through and know for what they are. But she had her own way of charm-ing: she was the being of infinite variety—to-day glad, to-morrow sad, freakish, and always exciting you by curiosity as to her next caprice, and so moody that after a season of the lowering weather of one of her dull humors you were ready to sacrifice something for the sake of the sunshine that she knew how to make so vivid and so sweet. Then, too, she brought forward her forces by detachment. At first she was the soul of domestic life, sitting at night beneath the light and embossing on weblike muslin designs of flower and leaf which she had learned in her convent, listening to Spencer as he read, and taking from the little wallet of her work-basket apropos scraps which she had preserved from the sermon of some Italian father of the Church or of some French divine. As for me, the only thing I knew was my poor music; and I used to burn with indignation when she interposed that unknown tongue between my husband and myself. Presently her horses came, and then, graceful in her dark riding-habit, she would spend a morning fearlessly subduing one of the fiery fellows, and dash away at last with plume and veil streaming behind her. In the early evening she would dance with the children—witch-dances they were—with her round arms linked above her head, and her feet weaving the measure in and out as deftly as any flashing-footed Bayadere³ might do—only when Spencer was there to see: at other times I saw she pushed the little hindering things aside without a glance.

By and by she began to display a strange dramatic sort of power: she would re-hearse to Spencer scenes that she had met with from day to day in the place, giving now the old churchwarden's voice and now the sexton's, their gestures and very faces; she could tell the ailments of half the old women in the parish who came to me with them, and in their own tone and manner to the life; she told us once of a street-scene, with the crier crying a lost child, the mother following with lamentations, the passing strangers questioning, the boys hooting, and the child's reappearance, fol-lowed by a tumult, with kisses and blows and cries, so that I thought I saw it all; and presently she had found the secret and vulnerable spot of every friend we had, and could personate them all as vividly as if she did it by necromancy.

One night she began to sketch our portraits in charcoal: the likenesses were not perfect; she exaggerated the careless elegance of Spencer's attitude; perhaps the primness of my own. But yet he saw there the ungraceful trait for the first time, I think. And so much led to more: she brought out her portfolios, and there were her pencil-sketches from the Rhine and from the Guadalquivir, rich water-colors of Venetian scenes, interiors of old churches, and sheet after sheet covered with details of church architecture. Spencer had been admiring all the others—in spite of

---

³ **Bayadere:** A dancing girl from India who dances before images of the gods.

something that I thought I saw in them, a something that was not true, a trait of her own identity, for I had come to criticise her sharply—but when his eye rested on those sheets I saw it sparkle, and he caught them up and pored over them one by one.

"I see you have mastered the whole thing," he said: "you must instruct me here." And so she did. And there were hours, while I was busied with servants and accounts or with the children, when she was closeted with Spencer in the study, criticising, comparing, making drawings, hunting up authorities; other hours when they walked away together to the site of the new church that was building, and here an arch was destroyed, and there an aisle was extended, and here a row of cloisters sketched into the plan, and there a row of windows, till the whole design was reversed and made over. And they had the thing between them, for, admire and sympathize as I might, I did not know. At first Spencer would repeat the day's achievement to me, but the contempt for my ignorance which she did not deign to hide soon put an end to it when she was present.

It was this interest that now unveiled a new phase of her character: she was devout. She had a little altar in her room; she knew all about albs and chasubles; she would have persuaded Spencer to burn candles in the chancel; she talked of a hundred mysteries and symbols; she wanted to embroider a stole to lay across his shoulders. She was full of small church sentimentalities, and as one after another she uttered them, it seemed to me that her belief was no sound fruit of any system—if it were belief, and not a mere bunch of fancies—but only, as you might say, a rotten windfall of the Romish Church: it had none of the round splendor of that Church's creed, none of the pure simplicity of ours: it would be no stay in trouble, no shield in temptation. I said as much to Spencer.

"You are prejudiced," said he: "her belief is the result of long observation abroad, I think. She has found the need of outward observances: they are, she has told me, a shrine to the body of her faith, like that commanded in the building of the tabernacle, where the ark of the covenant was enclosed in the holy of holies."

"And you didn't think it profane in her to speak so? But I don't believe it, Spencer," I said. "She has no faith: she has some sentimentalisms."

"You are prejudiced," he repeated. "She seems to me a wonderful and gifted being."

"Too gifted," I said. "Her very gifts are unnatural in their abundance. There must be scrofula there to keep such a fire in the blood and sting the brain to such action: she will die in a madhouse, depend upon it." Think of my saying such a thing as that!

"I have never heard you speak so before," he replied coldly. "I hope you do not envy her her powers."

"I envy her nothing," I cried. "For she is as false as she is beautiful!" But I did—oh I did!

"Beautiful?" said Spencer. "Is she beautiful? I never thought of that."

"You are very blind, then," I said with a glad smile.

Spencer smiled too. "It is not the kind of beauty I admire," said he.

"Then I must teach you, sir," said she. And we both started to see her in the doorway, and I, for one, did not know, till shortly before I found myself here, how much or how little she had learned of what we said.

"Then I must teach you, sir," said she again. And she came deliberately into the firelight and paused upon the rug, drew out the silver arrows and shook down all her hair about her, till the great snake-like coils unrolled upon the floor.

"Hyacinthine," said Spencer.

"Indeed it is," said she. "The very color of the jacinth, with that red tint in its darkness that they call black in the shade and gold in the sun. Now look at me."

"Shut your eyes, Spencer," I cried, and laughed.

But he did not shut his eyes. The firelight flashed over her: the color in her cheeks and on her lips sprang ripe and red in it as she held the hair away from them with her rosy finger-tips; her throat curved small and cream-white from the bosom that the lace of her dinner-dress scarcely hid; and the dark eyes glowed with a great light as they lay full on his.

"You mustn't call it vanity," said she. "It is only that it is impossible, looking at the picture in the glass, not to see it as I see any other picture. But for all that, I know it is not every fool's beauty: it is no daub for the vulgar gaze, but a masterpiece that it needs the educated eye to find. I could tell you how this nostril is like that in a famous marble, how the curve of this cheek is that of a certain Venus, the line of this forehead like the line in the dreamy Antinous'[4] forehead. Are you taught? Is it—?"

Then she twisted her hair again and fastened the arrows, and laughed and turned away to look over the evening paper. But as for Spencer, as he lay back in his lordly way, surveying the vision from crown to toe, I saw him flush—I saw him flush and start and quiver, and then he closed his eyes and pressed his fingers on them, and lay back again and said not a word.

She began to read aloud something concerning services at the recent dedication of a church. I was called out as she read. When I came back, a half hour afterward, they were talking. I stopped at my worktable in the next room for a skein of floss that she had asked me for, and I heard her saying, "You cannot expect me to treat you with reverence. You are a married priest, and you know what opinion I necessarily must have of married priests." Then I came in and she was silent.

But I knew, I always knew, that if Spencer had not felt himself weak, had not found himself stirred, if he had not recognized that, when he flushed and quivered before her charm, it was the flesh and not the spirit that tempted him, he would not have listened to her subtle invitation to austerity. As it was, he did. He did—partly in shame, partly in punishment; but to my mind the listening was confession. She had set the wedge that was to sever our union—the little seed in a mere idle cleft that grows and grows and splits the rock asunder.

Well, I had my duties, you know. I never felt my husband's wealth a reason why I should neglect them any more than another wife should neglect her duties. I was

---

[4] **Antinous:** Page of the Roman emperor Hadrian; thus, a model of male beauty.

wanted in the parish, sent for here and waited for there: the dying liked to see me comfort their living, the living liked to see me touch their dead; some wanted help, and others wanted consolation; and where I felt myself too young and unlearned to give advice, I could at least give sympathy. Perhaps I was the more called upon for such detail of duty because Spencer was busy with the greater things, the church-building and the sermons—sermons that once on a time lifted you and held you on their strong wings. But of late Spencer had been preaching old sermons. He had been moody and morose too: sometimes he seemed oppressed with melancholy. He had spoken to me strangely, had looked at me as if he pitied me, had kept away from me. But she had not regarded his moods: she had followed him in his solitary strolls, had sought him in his study; and she had ever a mystery or symbol to be interpreted, the picture of a private chapel that she had heard of when abroad, or the ground-plan of an ancient one, or some new temptation to his ambition, as I divine. And soon he was himself again.

I was wrong to leave him so to her, but what was there else for me to do? And as for those duties of mine, as I followed them I grew restive; I abridged them. I hastened home. I was impatient even with the detentions the children caused. I could not leave them to their nurses, for all that; but they kept me away from him, and he was alone with her.

One day at last he told me that his mind was troubled by the suspicion that his marriage was a mistake; that on his part at least it had been wrong; that he had been thinking a priest should have the Church only for his bride, and should wait at the altar mortified in every affection; that it was not for hands that were full of caresses and lips that were covered with kisses to touch the sacrament, to offer praise. But for answer I brought my children and put them in his arms. I was white and cold and shaking, but I asked him if they were not justification enough. And I told him that he did his duty better abroad for the heartening of a wife at home, and that he knew better how to interpret God's love to men through his own love for his children. And I laid my head on his breast beside them, and he clasped us all and we cried together, he and I.

But that was not enough, I found. And when our good bishop came, who had always been like a father to Spencer, I led the conversation to that point one evening, and he discovered Spencer's trouble, and took him away and reasoned with him. The bishop was a power with Spencer, and I think that was the end of it.

The end of that, but only the beginning of the rest. For she had accustomed him to the idea of separation from me—the idea of doing without me. He had put me away from himself once in his mind: we had been one soul, and now we were two.

One day, as I stood in my sleeping-room with the door ajar, she came in. She had never been there before, and I cannot tell you how insolently she looked about her. There was a bunch of flowers on a stand that Spencer himself placed there for me every morning. He had always done so, and there had been no reason for breaking off the habit; and I had always worn one of them at my throat. She advanced a hand to pull out a blossom. "Do not touch them," I cried: "my husband puts them there."

"Suppose he does," said she lightly. "For how long?" Then she overlooked me with a long sweeping glance of search and contempt, shrugged her shoulders, and with a French sentence that I did not understand turned back and coolly broke off the blossom she had marked and hung it in her hair. I could not take her by the shoulders and put her from the room. I could not touch the flowers that she had desecrated. I left the room myself, and left her in it, and went down to dinner for the first time without the flower at my throat. I saw Spencer's eye note the omission: perhaps he took it as a release from me, for he never put the flowers in my room again after that day.

Nor did he ask me any more into his study, as he had been used, or read his sermons to me. There was no need of his talking over the church-building with me—he had her to talk it over with. And as for our music, that had been a rare thing since she arrived, for her conversation had been such as to leave but little time for it, and somehow when she came into the music-room and began to dictate to me the time in which I should take an Inflammatus and the spirit in which I should sing a ballad, I could not bear it. Then, too, to tell you the truth, my voice was hoarse and choked with tears full half the time.

It was some weeks after the flowers ceased that our youngest child fell ill. She was very ill—I don't think Spencer knew how ill. I dared not trust her with any one, and Spencer said no one could take such care of her as her mother could; so, although we had nurses in plenty, I hardly left the room by night or day. I heard their voices down below, I saw them go out for their walks. It was a hard fight, but I saved her.

But I was worn to a shadow when all was done—worn with anxiety for her, with alternate fevers of hope and fear, with the weight of my responsibility as to her life; and with anxiety for Spencer too, with a despairing sense that the end of peace had come, and with the total sleeplessness of many nights. Now, when the child was mending and gaining every day, I could not sleep if I would.

The doctor gave me anodynes, but to no purpose: they only nerved me wide awake. My eyes ached, and my brain ached, and my body ached, but it was of no use: I could not sleep. I counted the spots on the wall, the motes upon my eyes, the notes of all the sheets of music I could recall. I remembered the Eastern punishment of keeping the condemned awake till they die, and wondered what my crime was; I thought if I could but sleep I might forget my trouble, or take it up freshly and master it. But no, it was always there—a heavy cloud, a horror of foreboding. As I heard that woman's step go by the door I longed to rid the house of it, and I dinted my palms with my nails till she had passed.

I did not know what to do. It seemed to me that I was wicked in letting the thing go on, in suffering Spencer to be any longer exposed to her power; but then I feared to take a step lest I should thereby rivet the chains she was casting on him. And then I longed so for one hour of the old dear happiness—the days when I and the children had been all and enough. I did not know what to do; I had no one to counsel with; I was wild within myself, and all distraught. Once I thought if I could not rid the house of her I could rid it of myself; and as I went through a dark passage and chanced to look up where a bright-headed nail glittered, I questioned if it would bear my weight. For days the idea haunted me. I fancied that when I was gone perhaps he would love me again, and at any rate I might be asleep and at rest. But the thought of the children prevented me, and one other thought—I was not certain that even my sorrows would excuse me before God.

I went down to dinner again at last. How she glowed and abounded in her beauty as she sat there! And I—I must have been very thin and ghastly: perhaps I looked a little wild in all my bewilderment and hurt. His heart smote him, it may be, for he came round to where I sat by the fire afterward and smoothed my hair and kissed my forehead. He could not tell all I was suffering then—all I was struggling with; for I thought I had better put him out of the world than let him, who was once so pure and good, stay in it to sin. I could have done it, you know. For though I still lay with the little girl, I could have stolen back into our own room with the chloroform, and he would never have known. I turned the handle of the door one night, but the bolt was slipped. I never thought of killing her, you see: let her live and sin, if she would. She was the thing of slime and sin, a splendid tropical growth of the passionate heat and the slime: it was only her nature. But then we think it no harm to kill reptiles, however splendid.

But it was by that time that the voices had begun to talk with me—all night long, all day. It was they, I found, that had kept me so sleepless. Go where I might, they were ever before me. If I went to the woods, I heard them in the whisper of every pine tree. If I went down to the seashore, I heard them in the plash of every wave. I heard them in the wind, in the singing of my ears, in the children's breath as I hung above them,—for I had decided that if I went out of the world I would take the children with me. If I sat down to play, the things would twist the chords into discords; if I sat down to read, they would come between me and the page.

Then I could see the creatures: they had wings like bats. I did not dare speak of them, although I fancied she suspected me, for once she said, as I was kissing my little girl, "When you are gone to a madhouse, don't think they'll have many such kisses." Did she say it? or did I think she said it? I did not answer her, I did not look up: I suppose I should have flown at her throat if I had.

I took the children out with me on my rambles: we went for miles; sometimes I carried one, sometimes the other. I took such long, long walks to escape those noisome things: they would never leave me till I was quite tired out. Now and then I was gone the whole day; and all the time that I was gone he was with her, I knew, and she was tricking out her beauty and practising her arts.

I went to a little festival with them, for Spencer insisted. And she made shadow-pictures on the wall, wonderful things with her perfect profile and her perfect arms and her subtle curves—she out of sight, the shadow only seen. Now it was Isis, I remember, and now it was the head and shoulders and trailing hair of a floating sea-nymph. And then there were charades in which she played; and I can't tell you the glorious thing she looked when she came on as Helen of Troy with all her "beauty shadowed in white veils," you know—that brown and red beauty with its smiles and radiance under the wavering of the flower-wrought veil. I sat by Spencer, and I felt him shiver. He was fighting and struggling too within himself, very likely; only he knew that he was going to yield after all—only he longed to yield while he feared. But as for me, I saw one of those bat-like things perched on her ear as she stood before us, and when she opened her mouth to speak I saw them flying in and out. And I said to Spencer, "She is tormenting me. I cannot stay and see her swallowing the souls of men in this way." And I would have gone, but he held me down fast in my seat. But if I was crazy then—as they say I was, I suppose—it was only with a metaphor, for she was sucking Spencer's soul out of his body.

But I was not crazy. I should admit I might have been if I alone had seen those evil spirits. But Spencer saw them too. He never told me so, but—there are subtle ways—I knew he did; for when I opened the church door late, as I often did at that time after my long walks, they would rush in past me with a whizz, and as I sat in the pew I would see him steadily avoid looking at me; and if he looked by any chance, he would turn so pale that I have thought he would drop where he stood; and he would redden afterward as though one had struck him. He knew then what I endured with them; but I was not the one to speak of it. Don't tell me that his color changed and he shuddered so because I sat there mumbling and nodding to myself. It was because he saw those things mopping and mowing beside me and whispering in my ear. Oh what loathsomeness the obscene creatures whispered! Foul quips and evil words I had never heard before, ribald songs and oaths; and I would clap my hands over my mouth to keep from crying out at them. Creatures of the imagination, you may say. It is possible. But they were so vivid that they seem real to me even now. I burn and tingle as I recall them. And how could I have imagined such sounds, such shapes, of things I had never heard or seen or dreamed?

And Spencer was very unhappy, I am sure. I was the mother of his children, and if he loved me no more, he had an old kindness for me still, and my distress distressed him. But for all that the glamour was on him, and he could not give up that woman and her beauty and her charm. Once or twice he may have thought about sending her away, but perhaps he could not bring himself to do it—perhaps he reflected it was too late, and now it was no matter. But every day she stayed he was the more like wax in her hands. Oh, he was weaker than water that is poured out. He was abandoning himself, and forgetting earth and heaven and hell itself, before a passion—a passion that soon would cloy, and then would sting.

It was the spring season: I had been out several hours. The sunset fell while I was in the wood, and the stars came out; and at one time I thought I would lie down there on last year's leaves and never get up again. But I remembered the children, and went home to them. They were in bed and asleep when I took off my shoes and opened the door of their room—breathing so sweetly and evenly, the little yellow heads close together on one pillow, their hands tossed about the coverlid, their parted lips, their rosy cheeks. I knelt to feel the warm breath on my own cold cheek, and then the voices began whispering again: "If only they never waked! they never waked!"

And all I could do was to spring to my feet and run from the room. I ran shoe-less down the great staircase and through the long hall. I thought I would go to Spencer and tell him all—all my sorrows, all the suggestions of the voices, and maybe in the endeavor to save me he would save himself. And I ran down the long dimly-lighted drawing-room, led by the sound I heard, to the music-room, whose doors were open just beyond. It was lighted only by the pale glimmer from the other room and by the moonlight through the painted panes. And I paused to listen to what I had never listened to there—the sound of the harp and a voice with it. Of course they had not heard me coming, and I hesitated and looked, and then I glided within the door and stood just by the open piano there.

She sat at the harp singing—the huge gilded harp. I did not know she sang—she had kept that for her last reserve—but she struck the harp so that it sang itself, like some great prisoned soul, and her voice followed it—oh so rich a voice! My own was white and thin, I felt, beside it. But mine had soared, and hers still clung to earth—a contralto sweet with honeyed sweetness—the sweetness of unstrained honey that has the earth-taste and the heavy blossom-dust yet in it—sweet, though it grew hoarse and trembling with passion. He sat in one of the great arm-chairs just before her: he was white with feeling, with rapture, with forgetfulness; his eyes shone like stars. He moved restlessly, a strange smile kindled all his face: he bent toward her, and the music broke off in the middle as they threw their arms around each other, and hung there lip to lip and heart to heart. And suddenly I crashed down both my hands on the keyboard before me, and stood and glared upon them.

And I never knew anything more till I woke up here.

And that is the whole of it. That is the puzzle of it—was it a horrid nightmare, an insane vision, or was it true? Was it true that I saw Spencer, my white, clean lover, my husband, a man of God, the father of our spotless babies,—was it true that I saw him so, or was it only some wild, vile conjuration of disease? Oh, I would be willing to have been crazed a lifetime, a whole lifetime, only to wake one moment before I died and find that that had never been!

Well, well, well! When time passed and I became more quiet, I told the doctor here about the voices—I never told him of Spencer or of her—and he bade me dismiss care. He said I was ill—excitement and sleeplessness had surcharged my nerves with that strange magnetic fluid that has worked so much mischief in the world. There was no organic disease, you see; only when my nerves were rested and right, my brain would be right. And the doctor gave me medicines and books and work, and when I saw the bat-like things again I was to go instantly to him. And after a little while I was not sure that I did see them. And in a little while longer they had ceased to come altogether. And I have had no more of them. I was on my parole then in the parlor, at the table, in the grounds. I felt that I was cured of whatever had ailed me: I could escape at any moment that I wished.

And it came Christmas time. A terrible longing for home overcame me—for my children. I thought of them at this time when I had been used to take such pains for their pleasure. I thought of the little empty stockings, the sad faces; I fancied I could hear them crying for me. I forgot all about my word of honor. It seemed to me that I should die, that I might as well die, if I could not see my little darlings, and hold them on my knees, and sing to them while the chimes were ringing in the Christmas Eve. And winter was here and there was so much to do for them. And I walked down the garden, and looked out at the gate, and opened it and went through. And I slept that night in a barn—so free, so free and glad! And the next day an old farmer and his sons, who thought they did me a service, brought me back, and of course I shrieked and raved. And so would you.

But since then I have been in this ward and a prisoner. I have my work, my amusement. I send such little things as I can make to my girls. I read. Sometimes of late I sing in the Sunday service. The place is a sightly place; the grounds, when we are taken out, are fine; the halls are spacious and pleasant.

Pleasant—but ah, when you have trodden them ten years!

And so, you see, if I were a clod, if I had no memory, no desires, if I had never been happy before, I might be happy now. I am confident the doctor thinks me well. But he has no orders to let me go. Sometimes it is so wearisome. And it might be worse if lately I had not been allowed a new service. And that is to try to make a woman smile who came here a year ago. She is a little woman, swarthy as a Malay, but her hair, that grows as rapidly as a fungus grows in the night, is whiter than leprosy: her eyebrows are so long and white that they veil and blanch her dark dim eyes; and she has no front teeth. A stone from a falling spire struck her from her horse, they say. The blow battered her and beat out reason and beauty. Her mind is dead: she remembers nothing, knows nothing; but she follows me about like a dog: she seems to want to do something for me, to propitiate me. All she ever says is to beg me to do her no harm. She will not go to sleep without my hand in hers. Sometimes, after long effort, I think there is a gleam of intelligence, but the doctor says there was once too much intelligence, and her case is hopeless.

Hopeless, poor thing!—that is an awful word: I could not wish it said for my worst enemy.

In spite of these ten years I cannot feel that it has yet been said for me.

If I am strange just now, it is only the excitement of seeing you, only the habit of the strange sights and sounds here. I should be calm and well enough at home. I sit and picture to myself that some time Spencer will come for me—will take me to my girls, my fireside, my music. I shall hear his voice, I shall rest in his arms, I shall be blest again. For, oh, Elizabeth, I do forgive him all!

Or if he will not dare to trust himself at first, I picture to myself how he will send another—some old friend who knew me before my trouble—who will see me and judge, and carry back report that I am all I used to be—some friend who will open the gates of heaven to me, or close the gates of hell upon me—who will hold my life and my fate.

If—oh if it should be you, Elizabeth!

—1872

## Marietta Holley 1836–1926

Although she is largely forgotten today, Marietta Holley established a long and success-ful career as the "female Mark Twain," a literary comedian who used dialect humor to advocate women's rights and satirize the follies of a society that tried to confine women to separate spheres. Her comic treatment of feminist issues appears in the full title of her first volume: *My Opinion and Betsey Bobbet's: Designed as a Beacon Light, to Guide Women to Life, Liberty and the Pursuit of Happiness, but Which May Be Read by Members of the Sterner Sect, Without Injury to Themselves or the Book* (1873). Holley adopted the deceptive pseudonym of "Josiah Allen's Wife" as an ironic commentary on the way soci-ety asks a woman to surrender her identity in marriage, but the good humor and com-mon sense of her main narrator, Samantha, never places women in a position of sub-mission. At her best, Holley provides a vigorous female voice in the largely male tradition of dialect humor and challenges all the forms of arrogance and bigotry that limit women. Holley took Samantha and her husband, Josiah, through 22 books, many of them in-volving travel to places that Holley herself never visited (including Europe and several world fairs). It is Samantha' strong sense of her own identity and the true meaning of right and wrong that usually saves Josiah and others from error and mishap.

The selection here is from Holley's first book and indicates the way in which Samantha's practical affirmation of feminine knowledge is juxtaposed to the foolish presumptions of Betsey Bobbet. In its humorous treatment of sexism as a disease that afflicts both women and men in a repressive society, "The 4th of July in Jones-ville" has much to say about gender roles in American society.

**Further Reading** Jane Curry, *Marietta Holley* (1996); Kate Winter, *Marietta Holley: Life with "Josiah Allen's Wife"* (1984).

# 4th of July in Jonesville

A few days before the 4th Betsey Bobbet come into oure house in the mornin' and says she,

"Have you heard the news?"

"No," says I pretty brief, for I was jest puttin' in the ingrediences to a six quart pan loaf of fruit cake, and on them occasions I want my mind cool and unruffled.

"Aspire Todd is goin' to deliver the oration," says she.

"Aspire Todd! Who's he?" says I cooly.

"Josiah Allen's wife," says she, "have you forgotten the sweet poem that thrilled us so in the Jonesville Gimblet a few weeks since?"

"I haint been thrilled by no poem," says I with an almost icy face pourin' in my melted butter.

"Then it must be that you have never seen it, I have it in my port money[1] and I will read it to you," says she, not heedin' the dark froun gatherin' on my eyebrow, and she begun to read,

A questioning sail sent over the Mystic Sea.

BY PROF. ASPIRE TODD.

So the majestic thunder-bolt of feeling,
Out of our inner lives, our unseen beings flow,
Vague dreams revealing.
Oh, is it so? Alas! or no,
How be it, Ah! how so ?

Is matter going to rule the deathless mind?
What is matter? Is it indeed so?
Oh, truths combined;
Do the Magaloi theoi still tower to and fro?
How do they move? How flow?

Monstrous, aeriform, phantoms sublime,
Come leer at me, and Cadmian teeth my soul gnaw,
Through chiliasms of time;
Transcendentaly and remorslessly gnaw;
By what agency? Is it a law?

Perish the vacueus in huge immensities;
Hurl the broad thunderbolt of feeling free,
The vision dies;
So lulls the bellowing surf, upon the mystic sea,
Is it indeed so? Alas! Oh me.

"How this sweet poem appeals to tender hearts," says Betsey as she concluded it.

"How it appeals to tender heads" says I almost coldly, measurin' out my cinnamon in a big spoon.

"Josiah Allen's wife, has not your soul never sailed on that mystical sea he so sweetly depictures?"

"Not an inch," says I firmly, "not an inch."

"Have you not never been haunted by sorrowful phantoms you would fain bury in oblivion's sea?"

Frontispiece from *Samantha Among the Brethren* by Josiah Allen's wife (Marietta Holley), Funk & Wagnalls, 1890.

---

[1] **port money:** Betsey Bobbet's mispronunciation of *portmanteau*, a pretentious way of referring to the bag in which she has placed the poem. Throughout the text, the misspellings of words may reflect the dialect of the speaker or a comic misspelling, such as the use of "their" for both "there" and "their." In general, the text affirms the dignity of Samantha's plain speech (even when ungrammatical) over both Betsey's and Aspire Todd's language, which is pretentious and nonsensical as well as ungrammatical. In this respect, the story is very characteristic of much of the period's dialect comedy.

"Not once," says I "not a phantom," and says I as I measured out my raisons and English currants, "if folks would work as I do, from mornin' till night and earn thier honest bread by the sweat of thier eyebrows, they wouldn't be tore so much by phantoms as they be; it is your shiftless creeters that are always bein' gored by phantoms, and havin' 'em leer at 'em," says I with my spectacles bent keenly on her, "Why don't they leer at me Betsey Bobbet?"

"Because you are intellectually blind, you cannot see."

"I see enough," says I, "I see more'n I want to a good deal of the time." In a dignified silence, I then chopped my raisons impressively and Betsey started for home.

The celebration was held in Josiah's sugar bush, and I meant to be on the ground in good season, for when I have jobs I dread, I am for takin' 'em by the forelock and grapplin' with 'em at once. But as I was bakin' my last plum puddin' and chicken pie, the folks begun to stream by, I hadn't no idee thier could be so many folks scairt up in Jonesville. I thought to myself, I wonder if they'd flock out so to a prayer-meetin.' But they kep' a comin', all kind of folks, in all kinds of vehicles, from a 6 horse team, down to peacible lookin' men and wimmen drawin' baby wagons, with two babies in most of 'em.

There was a stagin' built in most the middle of the grove for the leadin' men of Jonesville, and some board seats all round it for the folks to set on. As Josiah owned the ground, he was invited to set upon the stagin'.

And as I glanced up at that man every little while through the day, I thought proudly to myself, there may be nobler lookin' men there, and men that would weigh more by the steelyards, but there haint a whiter shirt bosom there than Josiah Allen's.

When I got there the seats was full. Betsey Bobbet was jest ahead of me, and says she,

"Come on, Josiah Allen's wife, let us have a seat, we can obtain one, if we push and scramble enough." As I looked upon her carryin' out her doctrine, pushin' and scramblin', I thought to myself, if I didn't know to the contrary, I never should take you for a modest dignifier and retirer. And as I beheld her breathin' hard, and her elboes wildly wavin' in the air, pushin' in between native men of Jonesville and foreigners, I again methought, I don't believe you would be so sweaty and out of breath a votin' as you be now. And as I watched her labors and efforts I continued to methink sadly, how strange! how strange! that retirin' modesty and delicacy can stand so firm in some situations, and then be so quickly overthrowed in others seemin'ly not near so hard.

Betsey finally got a seat, wedged in between a large healthy Irishman and a native constable, and she motioned for me to come on, at the same time pokin' a respectable old gentleman in front of her, with her parasol, to make him move along. Says I,

"I may as well die one way as another, as well expier a standin' up, as in tryin' to get a seat," and I quietly leaned up against a hemlock tree and composed myself for events. A man heard my words which I spoke about 1-2 to myself, and says he,

"Take my seat, mum."

Says I "No! keep it."

Says he "I am jest comin' down with a fit, I have got to leave the ground instantly."

Says I "In them cases I will." So I sot. His tongue seemed thick, and his breath smelt of brandy, but I make no insinuations.

About noon Prof. Aspire Todd walked slowly on to the ground, arm in arm with the editor of the Gimlet, old Mr. Bobbet follerin' him closely behind. Countin' 2 eyes to a person, and the exceptions are triflin', there was 700 and fifty or sixty eyes aimed at him as he walked through the crowd. He was dressed in a new shinin' suit of black, his complexion was deathly, his hair was jest turned from white, and was combed straight back from his forward and hung down long, over his coat coller. He had a big moustache, about the color of his hair, only bearin' a little more on the sandy, and a couple of pale blue eyes with a pair of spectacles over 'em.

As he walked upon the stagin' behind the Editer of the Gimlet, the band struck up, "Hail to the chief, that in trihump advances." As soon as it stopped playin' the Editer of the Gimlet come forward and said—

"Fellow citizens of Jonesville and the adjacent and surroundin' world, I have the honor and privilege of presenting to you the orator of the day, the noble and eloquent Prof. Aspire Todd Esq.

Prof. Todd came forward and made a low bow.

"Bretheren and sisters of Jonesville" says he; "Friends and patrons of Liberty, in risin' upon this aeroter, I have signified by that act, a desire and a willingness to address you. I am not here fellow and sister citizens, to outrage your feelings by triflin' remarks, I am not here male patrons of liberty to lead your noble, and you female patrons your tender footsteps into the flowery fields of useless rhetorical eloquence; I am here noble brothers and sisters of Jonesville not in a mephitical manner, and I trust not in a mentorial, but to present a few plain truths in a plain manner, for your consideration. My friends we are in one sense but tennifolious blossoms of life; or, if you will pardon the tergiversation, we are all but mineratin' tennirosters, hovering upon an illinition of mythoplasm."

"Jess so," cried old Bobbet who was settin' on a bench right under the speaker's stand, with his fat red face lookin' up shinin' with pride and enthusiasm, (and the brandy he had took to honor the old Revolutionary heroes) "Jess so! so we be!"

Prof. Todd looked down on him in a troubled kind of a way for a minute, and then went on—

"Noble inhabitants of Jonesville and the rural districts, we are actinolitic bein's, each of our souls, like the acalphia, radiates a circle of prismatic tentacles, showing the divine irridescent essence of which composed are they."

"Jes' so," shouted old Bobbet louder than before. "Jes' so, so they did, I've always said so."

"And if we are content to moulder out our existence, like fibrous, veticulated, polypus, clingin' to the crustaceous courts of custom, if we cling not like soarin' prytanes to the phantoms that lower thier sceptres down through the murky waves of retrogression, endeavorin' to lure us upward in the scale of progressive bein'—in what degree do we differ from the accolphia?"

"Jes' so," says old Bobbet, lookin' defiantly round on the audience. "There he has got you, how can they?"

Prof. Todd stopped again, looked doun on Bobbet, and put his hand to his brow in a wild kind of a way, for a minute, and then went on.

"Let us, noble brethren in the broad field of humanity, let us rise, let us prove that mind is superior to matter, let us prove ourselves superior to the acalphia—"

"Yes, less," says old Bobbet, "less prove ourselves." in the air in a rapped eloquence, and beatin' his breast in the same he cried,

"Shall these weak, helpless angels, these seraphines, these sweet, delicate, cooin' doves—whose only mission it is to sweetly coo—these rainbows, these posys vote? Never! my bretheren, never will we put such hardships upon 'em."

As he sot down, he professed himself and all the rest of his sect ready to die at any time, and in any way wimmin should say, rather than they should vote, or have any other hardship. Betsey Bobbet wept aloud, she was so delighted with it.

Jest as they concluded thier frantic cheers over his speech, a thin, feeble lookin' woman come by where I stood, drawin' a large baby wagon with two children in it, seemin'ly a two-year-old, and a yearlin'. She also carried one in her arms who was lame. She looked so beat out and so ready to drop down, that I got up and give her my seat, and says I,

"You look ready to fall down."

"Am I too late," says she, "to hear my husband's speech?"

"Is that your husband," says I, "that is laughin' and talkin' with that pretty girl?"

"Yes," says she with a sort of troubled look.

"Well, he jest finished."

She looked ready to cry, and as I took the lame child from her breakin' arms, says I—

"This is too hard for you."

"I wouldn't mind gettin' 'em on to the ground," says she, "I haint had only three miles to bring 'em that wouldn't be much if it wasn't for the work I had to do before I come."

"What did you have to do?" says I in pityin' accents.

"Oh, I had to fix him off, brush his clothes and black his boots, and then I did up all my work, and then I had to go out and make six length of fence—the cattle broke into the corn yesterday, and he was busy writin' his piece, and couldn't fix it—and then I had to mend his coat," glancin' at a thick coat in the wagon. "He didn't know but he should want it to wear home, he knew he was goin' to make a great effort, and thought he should sweat some, he is dreadful easy to take cold," says she with a worried look.

"Why didn't he help you along with the children?" says I, in a indignant tone.

"Oh, he said he had to make a great exertion to-day, and he wanted to have his mind free and clear; he is one of the kind that can't have their minds trammeled."

"It would do him good to be trammeled—hard!" says I, lookin' darkly on him.

"Don't speak so of him," says she beseechingly.

"Are you satisfied with his doin's?" says I, lookin' keenly at her.

"Oh yes," says she in a trustin' tone, liftin' her care-worn, weary countenance to mine, "oh yes, you don't know how beautiful he can *talk*."

I said no more, for it is a invincible rule of my life, not to make no disturbances in families. But I give the yearlin' pretty near a pound of candy on the spot, and the glances I cast on *him* and the pretty girl he was a flirtin' with, was cold enough to freeze 'em both into a male and female glazier.

Lawyer Nugentnow got up and said, "That whereas the speaking was foreclosed, or in other words finished, he motioned they should adjourn to the dinner table, as the fair committee had signified by a snowy signal that fluttered like a dove of promise above waves of emerald, or in plainer terms by a *towel*, that dinner was forthcoming; whereas he motioned that they should adjourn *sine die*[2] to the aforesaid table."

Old Mr. Bobbet, and the Editer of the Gimlet seconded the motion at the same time. And Shakespeare Bobbet wantin' to do somethin' in a public way, got up and motioned "that they proceed to the table on the usial road", but there wasn't any other way—only to wade the creek—that didn't seem to be necessary, but nobody took no notice of it, so it was jest as well.

The dinner was good, but there was an awful crowd round the tables, and I was glad I wore my old lawn dress, for the children was thick, and so was bread and butter, and sass of all kinds, and jell tarts And I hain't no shirk, I jost plunged right into the heat of the battle, as you may say, waitin' on the children, and the spots on my dress skirt would have been too much for anybody that couldn't count 40. To say nothin' about old Mr. Peedick steppin' through the back breadth, and Betsey Bobbet ketchin' holt of me, and rippin' it off the waist as much as 1-2 a yard. And then a horse started up behind the widder Tubbs, as I was bendin' down in front of her to get somethin' out of a basket, and she weighin' above 200, was precipitated onto my straw bonnet, jammin' it down almost as flat as it was before it was braided. I came off pretty well in other respects, only about two yards of the ruflin' of my black silk cape was tore by two boys who got to fightin' behind me, and bein' blind with rage tore it off, thinkin' they had got holt of each other's hair. There was a considerable number of toasts drank, I cant remember all of 'em, but among 'em was these,

"The eagle of Liberty; May her quills lengthen till the proud shadow of her wings shall sweetly rest on every land."

"The 4th of July; the star which our old four fathers tore from the ferocious mane of the howling lion of England, and set in the calm and majestic brow of *E pluribus unum*. May it gleam with brighter and brighter radience, till the lion shall hide his dazzled eyes, and cower like a stricken lamb at the feet of *E pluribus*."

---

[2] *sine die*: They adjourn without setting another time for reconvening; another example of the pretentious language that Holley mocks.

"Dr. Bombus our respected citizen; how he tenderly ushers us into a world of trial, and professionally and scientifically assists us out of it. May his troubles be as small as his morphine powders, and the circle of his joys as well rounded as his pills."

"The press of Jonesville, the Gimlet, and the Augur; May they perforate the crust of ignorance with a gigantic hole, through which blushing civilization can sweetly peer into futurity."

"The fair sect: first in war, first in peace, and first in the hearts of their country-men. May them that love the aforesaid, flourish like a green bayberry tree, whereas may them that hate them, dwindle down as near to nothin' as the bonnets of the aforesaid."

That peice of toast was Lawer Nugent's.

Prof. Aspire Todd's was the last.

"The Lumineus Lamp of Progression, whose sciatherical shadows falling upon earthly matter, not promoting sciolism, or Siccity, may it illumine humanity as it tar-digradely floats from matter's aquius wastes, to minds majestic and apyrous climes."

Shakspeare Bobbet then rose up, and says he,

"Before we leave this joyous grove I have a poem which I was requested to read to you, it is dedicated to the Goddess of Liberty, and was transposed by another fe-male, who modestly desires her name not to be mentioned any further than the initials B. B."

He then read the follerin' spirited lines:

Before all causes East or West,
I love the Liberty cause the best,
I love its cheerful greetings;
No joys on earth can e'er be found,
Like those pure pleasures that abound,
At Jonesville Liberty meetings.

To all the world I give my hand,
My heart is with that noble band,
The Jonesville Liberty brothers;
May every land preserved be,
Each clime that dotes on Liberty—
Jonesville before all others.

The picknick never broke up till most night, I went home a little while before it broke, and if there was a beat out creeter, I was; I jest dropped my delapidated form into a rockin' chair with a red cushien and says I,

"There needn't be another word said, I will never go to another 4th as long as my name is Josiah Allen's wife."

"You haint patriotic enough Semantha says Josiah, you dont love your country."

"What good has it done the nation to have me all tore to pieces? says I, "Look at my dress, look at my bonnet and cape, any one ought to be a iron clad to stand it, look at my dishes!" says I.

"I guess the old heroes of the Revolution went through more than that," says Josiah.

"Well I haint a old hero!" says I coolly.

"Well you can honor 'em cant you?"

"Honor 'em! Josiah Allen what good has it done to old Mr. Layfayette to have my new earthern pie plates smashed to bits, and a couple of tines broke off of one of my best forks? What good has it done to old Thomas Jefferson, to have my lawn dress tore off of me by Betsey Bobbet? what benefit has it been to John Adams, or Isaac Putnam to have old Peedick step through it? what honor has it been to George Washington to have my straw bonnet flatted down tight to my head? I am sick of this talk about honorin, and liberty and duty, I am sick of it," says I "folks will make a pack horse of duty, and ride it to circus'es and bull fights, if we had 'em. You may talk about honorin' the old heroes and goin' through all these performances to please 'em. But if they are in Heaven they can get along without heerin' the Jonesville brass band, and if they haint, they are probably where fire works haint much of a rarity to 'em."

Josiah quailed before my lofty tone and I relapsed into a weary and delapidated silence.

—1873

## Thomas Bailey Aldrich 1836–1907

Thomas Bailey Aldrich was a true New England son of Portsmouth, New Hampshire, renamed "Rivermouth" in *The Story of a Bad Boy* (1869–1870), his most important work, and elsewhere. Returning to New England after eight years in New York and New Orleans (1841–1849), Aldrich planned to attend Harvard and to apprentice himself to Longfellow, but his father's death dashed these hopes. While clerking in his uncle's counting house in New York City from 1852 to 1855, he wrote verse that was readily published in popular periodicals, touching on such subjects as a Hashish "trip," Islam versus Christianity ("The Crescent and the Cross"), and the anonymity of death in his widely recognized "Identity." After *The Bells: A Collection of Chimes* appeared in 1855, Aldrich committed himself to a literary life, first as a junior literary critic on N. P. Willis's *The Evening Mirror* at the age of nineteen, and later as an editor of newspapers and periodicals appealing to the large popular audience of the time. He was an editor for the rest of his life, as well as an admired essayist, poet, and fiction writer.

*Marjorie Daw and Other People* (1873) was most notable for the title story, an epistolary revelation of character which brilliantly constructed the title figure to turn with a twist that exposed the psychology of the other characters in a Jamesian manner. Admired in America and abroad as a comic achievement, it popularized the surprise ending and secured Aldrich his place among major short story writers.

*Two Bites at a Cherry and Other Tales* (1893) collected more of his short fiction; the psychological portraiture of the title story was often admired. The eight-volume collection of his works was published in 1897 and enlarged in 1907. As testimony to his place in American letters, the greatest writers of the era assembled at his funeral in 1907.

**Further Reading** Mrs. Thomas Bailey Aldrich, *Crowding Memories* (1920); Ferris Greenslet, *The Life of Thomas Bailey Aldrich* (1908); Samuel I. Bellman, "Thomas Bailey Aldrich" in *Dictionary of Literary Biography: American Short-Story Writers Before 1880*, Volume 74: 3–14 (1988); Charles E. Samuels, *Thomas Bailey Aldrich* (1965).

—*David E. E. Sloane, University of New Haven*

# Marjorie Daw

## I. Dr. Dillon to Edward Delaney, Esq., at The Pines, near Rye, N. H.

AUGUST 8, 187—.

Thomas Fogarty (1873–1938) provided a pen-and-ink drawing of "Marjorie Daw" for the 1899 edition of Aldrich's collected works.
*Courtesy Library of Congress Prints and Photographs Division, Washington D.C.*

MY DEAR SIR: I am happy to assure you that your anxiety is without reason. Flemming will be confined to the sofa for three or four weeks, and will have to be careful at first how he uses his leg. A fracture of this kind is always a tedious affair. Fortunately, the bone was very skilfully set by the surgeon who chanced to be in the drug-store where Flemming was brought after his fall, and I apprehend no permanent inconvenience from the accident. *Flemming is doing perfectly well physically;* but I must confess that the irritable and morbid state of mind into which he has fallen causes me a great deal of uneasiness. He is the last man in the world who ought to break his leg. You know how impetuous our friend is ordinarily, what a soul of restlessness and energy, never content unless he is rushing at some object, like a sportive bull at a red shawl; but amiable withal. He is no longer amiable. His temper has become something frightful. Miss Fanny Flemming came up from Newport, where the family are staying for the summer, to nurse him; but he packed her off the next morning in tears. He has a complete set of Balzac's works, twenty-seven volumes, piled up near his sofa, to throw at Watkins whenever that exemplary serving-man appears with his meals. Yesterday I very innocently brought Flemming a small basket of lemons. You know it was a strip of lemon-peel on the curbstone that caused our friend's mischance. Well, he no sooner set his eyes upon these lemons than he fell into such a rage as I cannot adequately describe. This is only one of his moods, and the least distressing. At other times he sits with bowed head regarding his splintered limb, silent, sullen, despairing. When this fit is on him—and it sometimes lasts all day—nothing can distract his melancholy. He refuses to eat, does not even read the newspapers; books, except as projectiles for Watkins, have no charms for him. His state is truly pitiable.

Now, if he were a poor man, with a family depending on his daily labor, this irritability and despondency would be natural enough. But in a young fellow of twenty-four, with plenty of money and seemingly not a care in the world, the thing is monstrous. If he continues to give way to his vagaries in this manner, he will end by bringing on an inflammation of the fibula. It was the fibula he broke. I am at my wits' end to know what to prescribe for him. I have anæsthetics and lotions, to make people sleep and to soothe pain; but I've no medicine that will make a man have a little common-sense. That is beyond my skill, but maybe it is not beyond yours. You are Flemming's intimate friend, his *fidus Achates*.[1] Write to him, write to him frequently, distract his mind, cheer him up, and prevent him from becoming a confirmed case of melancholia. Perhaps he has some important plans disarranged by his present confinement. If he has you will know, and will know how to advise him judiciously. I trust your father finds the change beneficial? I am, my dear sir, with great respect, etc.

## II. Edward Delaney to John Flemming, West 38th Street, New York.

August 9,—.

My dear Jack: I had a line from Dillon this morning, and was rejoiced to learn that your hurt is not so bad as reported. Like a certain personage, you are not so black and blue as you are painted. Dillon will put you on your pins again in two or three weeks, if you will only have patience and follow his counsels. Did you get my note of last Wednesday? I was greatly troubled when I heard of the accident.

I can imagine how tranquil and saintly you are with your leg in a trough! It is deuced awkward, to be sure, just as we had promised ourselves a glorious month together at the seaside; but we must make the best of it. It is unfortunate, too, that my father's health renders it impossible for me to leave him. I think he has much improved; the sea air is his native element; but he still needs my arm to lean upon in his walks, and requires some one more careful than a servant to look after him. I cannot come to you, dear Jack, but I have hours of unemployed time on hand, and I will write you a whole post-office full of letters if that will divert you. Heaven knows, I have n't anything to write about. It is n't as if we were living at one of the beach

---

[1] *fidus Achates*: Latin for "faithful Achates," Aeneas's companion; a trustworthy friend.

houses; then I could do you some character studies, and fill your imagination with groups of sea-goddesses, with their (or somebody else's) raven and blond manes hanging down their shoulders. You should have Aphrodite in morning wrapper, in evening costume, and in her prettiest bathing suit. But we are far from all that here. We have rooms in a farm-house, on a cross-road, two miles from the hotels, and lead the quietest of lives.

I wish I were a novelist. This old house, with its sanded floors and high wainscots, and its narrow windows looking out upon a cluster of pines that turn themselves into æolian-harps[2] every time the wind blows, would be the place in which to write a summer romance. It should be a story with the odors of the forest and the breath of the sea in it. It should be a novel like one of that Russian fellow's,—what's his name?— Tourguénieff, Turguenef, Turgenif, Toorguniff, Turgénjew,—nobody knows how to spell him. Yet I wonder if even a Liza or an Alexandra Paulovna[3] could stir the heart of a man who has constant twinges in his leg. I wonder if one of our own Yankee girls of the best type, haughty and *spirituelle*, would be of any comfort to you in your present deplorable condition. If I thought so, I would hasten down to the Surf House and catch one for you; or, better still, I would find you one over the way.

Picture to yourself a large white house just across the road, nearly opposite our cottage. It is not a house, but a mansion, built, perhaps, in the colonial period, with rambling extensions, and gambrel roof, and a wide piazza on three sides,—a self-possessed, high-bred piece of architecture, with its nose in the air. It stands back from the road, and has an obsequious retinue of fringed elms and oaks and weeping willows. Sometimes in the morning, and oftener in the afternoon, when the sun has withdrawn from that part of the mansion, a young woman appears on the piazza with some mysterious Penelope web of embroidery[4] in her hand, or a book. There is a hammock over there,—of pineapple fibre, it looks from here. A hammock is very becoming when one is eighteen, and has golden hair, and dark eyes, and an emerald-colored illusion dress looped up after the fashion of a Dresden china shepherdess, and is *chaussée*[5] like a belle of the time of Louis Quatorze. All this splendor goes into that hammock, and sways there like a pond-lily in the golden afternoon. The window of my bedroom looks down on that piazza,—and so do I.

But enough of this nonsense, which ill becomes a sedate young attorney taking his vacation with an invalid father. Drop me a line, dear Jack, and tell me how you really are. State your case. Write me a long, quiet letter. If you are violent or abusive, I'll take the law to you.

---

[2] **æolian-harps:** Musical instruments played by the wind.

[3] **a Liza or an Alexandra Paulovna:** The major characters, respectively, in the novels *Liza: A Nest of Nobles* (1856) and *Rudin* (1856) by the Russian novelist, Ivan Turgenev (1818–1883).

[4] **Penelope web of embroidery:** In Homer's *Odyssey*, Penelope remains faithful to her absent husband by telling her suitors that she cannot marry until she finishes weaving a shroud. Each night she unravels what she has woven during the day.

[5] *chaussée:* Provided with shoes and stockings.

## III. John Flemming to Edward Delaney.

August 11,—.

Your letter, dear Ned, was a godsend. Fancy what a fix I am in,—I, who never had a day's sickness since I was born. My left leg weighs three tons. It is embalmed in spices and smothered in layers of fine linen, like a mummy. I can't move. I have n't moved for five thousand years. I'm of the time of Pharaoh.

I lie from morning till night on a lounge, staring into the hot street. Everybody is out of town enjoying himself. The brown-stone-front houses across the street resemble a row of particularly ugly coffins set up on end. A green mould is settling on the names of the deceased, carved on the silver door-plates. Sardonic spiders have sewed up the key-holes. All is silence and dust and desolation.—I interrupt this a moment, to take a shy at Watkins with the second volume of César Birotteau. Missed him! I think I could bring him down with a copy of Sainte-Beuve or the Dictionnaire Universel, if I had it. These small Balzac books somehow don't quite fit my hand; but I shall fetch him yet. I've an idea Watkins is tapping the old gentleman's Château Yquem.[6] Duplicate key of the wine-cellar. Hibernian swarries[7] in the front basement. Young Cheops up stairs, snug in his cerements.[8] Watkins glides into my chamber, with that colorless, hypocritical face of his drawn out long like an accordion; but I know he grins all the way down stairs, and is glad I have broken my leg. Was not my evil star in the very zenith when I ran up to town to attend that dinner at Delmonico's? I did n't come up altogether for that. It was partly to buy Frank Livingstone's roan mare Margot. And now I shall not be able to sit in the saddle these two months. I'll send the mare down to you at The Pines,—is that the name of the place?

Old Dillon fancies that I have something on my mind. He drives me wild with lemons. Lemons for a mind diseased! Nonsense. I am only as restless as the devil under this confinement,—a thing I'm not used to. Take a man who has never had so much as a headache or a toothache in his life, strap one of his legs in a section of water-spout, keep him in a room in the city for weeks, with the hot weather turned on, and then expect him to smile and purr and be happy! It is preposterous. I can't be cheerful or calm.

Your letter is the first consoling thing I have had since my disaster, ten days ago. It really cheered me up for half an hour. Send me a screed, Ned, as often as you can, if you love me. Anything will do. Write me more about that little girl in the hammock. That was very pretty, all that about the Dresden china shepherdess and the pond-lily; the imagery a little mixed, perhaps, but very pretty. I did n't suppose you had so much sentimental furniture in your upper story. It shows how one may be familiar for years

---

[6] **Château Yquem:** A type of wine.
[7] **Hibernian swarries:** Irish parties; swarries is a comic pronunciation of soirees.

[8] **Young Cheops … cerements:** An Egyptian pharaoh in the cloth used to wrap the dead.

with the reception-room of his neighbor, and never suspect what is directly under his mansard. I supposed your loft stuffed with dry legal parchments, mortgages and affidavits; you take down a package of manuscript, and lo! there are lyrics and sonnets and canzonettas. You really have a graphic descriptive touch, Edward Delaney, and I suspect you of anonymous love-tales in the magazines.

I shall be a bear until I hear from you again. Tell me all about your pretty *inconnue* across the road. What is her name? Who is she ? Who's her father ? Where's her mother? Who's her lover ? You cannot imagine how this will occupy me. The more trifling the better. My imprisonment has weakened me intellectually to such a degree that I find your epistolary gifts quite considerable. I am passing into my second childhood. In a week or two I shall take to India-rubber rings and prongs of coral. A silver cup, with an appropriate inscription, would be a delicate attention on your part. In the mean time, write!

## IV. EDWARD DELANEY TO JOHN FLEMMING.

AUGUST 12,——.

THE sick pasha shall be amused. *Bismillah!*[9] he wills it so. If the story-teller becomes prolix and tedious,—the bow-string and the sack, and two Nubians to drop him into the Piscataqua! But, truly, Jack, I have a hard task. There is literally nothing here,— except the little girl over the way. She is swinging in the hammock at this moment. It is to me compensation for many of the ills of life to see her now and then put out a small kid boot, which fits like a glove, and set herself going. Who is she, and what is her name? Her name is Daw. Only daughter of Mr. Richard W. Daw, ex-colonel and banker. Mother dead. One brother at Harvard, elder brother killed at the battle of Fair Oaks, nine years ago. Old, rich family, the Daws. This is the homestead, where father and daughter pass eight months of the twelve; the rest of the year in Baltimore and Washington. The New England winter too many for the old gentleman. The daughter is called Marjorie,—Marjorie Daw. Sounds odd at first, does n't it ? But after you say it over to yourself half a dozen times, you like it. There's a pleasing quaintness to it, something prim and violet-like. Must be a nice sort of girl to be called Marjorie Daw.

I had mine host of The Pines in the witness-box last night, and drew the foregoing testimony from him. He has charge of Mr. Daw's vegetable-garden, and has known the family these thirty years. Of course I shall make the acquaintance of my neighbors before many days. It will be next to impossible for me not to meet Mr. Daw or Miss Daw in some of my walks. The young lady has a favorite path to the sea-beach. I shall intercept her some morning, and touch my hat to her. Then the princess will bend her fair head to me with courteous surprise not unmixed with haughtiness. Will snub me, in fact. All this for thy sake, O Pasha of the Snapt Axle-tree!.... How oddly things fall out! Ten minutes ago I was called down to the par-

---

[9] *Bismillah!*: The opening phrase of each section of the Koran, meaning "In the name of Allah!"

lor,—you know the kind of parlors in farmhouses on the coast, a sort of amphibi-ous parlor, with sea-shells on the mantel-piece and spruce branches in the chimney-place,—where I found my father and Mr. Daw doing the antique polite to each other. He had come to pay his respects to his new neighbors. Mr. Daw is a tall, slim gentleman of about fifty-five, with a florid face and snow-white mustache and side-whiskers. Looks like Mr. Dombey,[10] or as Mr. Dombey would have looked if he had served a few years in the British Army. Mr. Daw was a colonel in the late war, commanding the regiment in which his son was a lieutenant. Plucky old boy, back-bone of New Hampshire granite. Before taking his leave, the colonel delivered him-self of an invitation as if he were issuing a general order. Miss Daw has a few friends coming, at 4 P. M., to play croquet on the lawn (parade-ground) and have tea (cold rations) on the piazza. Will we honor them with our company? (or be sent to the guard-house.) My father declines on the plea of ill-health. My father's son bows with as much suavity as he knows, and accepts.

In my next I shall have something to tell you. I shall have seen the little beauty face to face. I have a presentiment, Jack, that this Daw is a *rara avis!*[11] Keep up your spirits, my boy, until I write you another letter,—and send me along word how's your leg.

## V. Edward Delaney to John Flemming.

AUGUST 13,—.

THE party, my dear Jack, was as dreary as possible. A lieutenant of the navy, the rec-tor of the Episcopal church at Stillwater, and a society swell from Nahant. The lieu-tenant looked as if he had swallowed a couple of his buttons, and found the bullion rather indigestible; the rector was a pensive youth, of the daffydowndilly sort; and the swell from Nahant was a very weak tidal wave indeed. The women were much better, as they always are; the two Miss Kingsburys of Philadelphia, staying at the Sea-shell House, two bright and engaging girls. But Marjorie Daw!

The company broke up soon after tea, and I remained to smoke a cigar with the colonel on the piazza. It was like seeing a picture to see Miss Marjorie hovering around the old soldier, and doing a hundred gracious little things for him. She brought the cigars and lighted the tapers with her own delicate fingers, in the most enchanting fashion. As we sat there, she came and went in the summer twilight, and seemed, with her white dress and pale gold hair, like some lovely phantom that had sprung into existence out of the smoke-wreaths. If she had melted into air, like the statue of Galatea in the play,[12] I should have been more sorry than surprised.

---

[10] **Mr. Dombey:** Character in Charles Dickens's *Dombey and Sons* (1848).
[11] *rara avis:* A rare bird.
[12] **Galatea in the play:** The name given to Pygmalian's wife by a post-classical author. In Ovid's *Metamorphosis,*

Pygmalian falls in love with the statue of a woman he has created, and Aphrodite brings her to life so the two can marry. The success of W. S. Gilbert's play *Pygmalian and Galatea* in 1871 inspired a number of other dra-matic versions over the next few years.

It was easy to perceive that the old colonel worshipped her, and she him. I think the relation between an elderly father and a daughter just blooming into womanhood the most beautiful possible. There is in it a subtle sentiment that cannot exist in the case of mother and daughter, or that of son and mother. But this is getting into deep water.

I sat with the Daws until half past ten, and saw the moon rise on the sea. The ocean, that had stretched motionless and black against the horizon, was changed by magic into a broken field of glittering ice, interspersed with marvellous silvery fjords. In the far distance the Isles of Shoals loomed up like a group of huge bergs drifting down on us. The Polar Regions in a June thaw! It was exceedingly fine. What did we talk about? We talked about the weather—and *you!* The weather has been disagreeable for several days past,—and so have you. I glided from one topic to the other very naturally. I told my friends of your accident; how it had frustrated all our summer plans, and what our plans were. I played quite a spirited solo on the fibula. Then I described you; or, rather, I did n't. I spoke of your amiability, of your patience under this severe affliction; of your touching gratitude when Dillon brings you little presents of fruit; of your tenderness to your sister Fanny, whom you would not allow to stay in town to nurse you, and how you heroically sent her back to Newport, preferring to remain alone with Mary, the cook, and your man Watkins, to whom, by the way, you were devotedly attached. If you had been there, Jack, you would n't have known yourself. I should have excelled as a criminal lawyer, if I had not turned my attention to a different branch of jurisprudence.

Miss Marjorie asked all manner of leading questions concerning you. It did not occur to me then, but it struck me forcibly afterwards, that she evinced a singular interest in the conversation. When I got back to my room, I recalled how eagerly she leaned forward, with her full, snowy throat in strong moonlight, listening to what I said. Positively, I think I made her like you!

Miss Daw is a girl whom you would like immensely, I can tell you that. A beauty without affectation, a high and tender nature,—if one can read the soul in the face. And the old colonel is a noble character, too.

I am glad the Daws are such pleasant people. The Pines is an isolated spot, and my resources are few. I fear I should have found life here somewhat monotonous before long, with no other society than that of my excellent sire. It is true, I might have made a target of the defenceless invalid; but I have n't a taste for artillery, *moi.*

## VI. John Flemming to Edward Delaney.

August 17,—.

For a man who has n't a taste for artillery, it occurs to me, my friend, you are keeping up a pretty lively fire on my inner works. But go on. Cynicism is a small brass field-piece that eventually bursts and kills the artilleryman.

You may abuse me as much as you like, and I'll not complain; for I don't know what I should do without your letters. They are curing me. I have n't hurled anything at Watkins since last Sunday, partly because I have grown more amiable under your teaching, and partly because Watkins captured my ammunition one night, and carried it off to the library. He is rapidly losing the habit he had acquired of dodging whenever I rub my ear, or make any slight motion with my right arm. He is still suggestive of the wine-cellar, however. You may break, you may shatter Watkins, if you will, but the scent of the Roederer[13] will hang round him still.

Ned, that Miss Daw must be a charming person. I should certainly like her. I like her already. When you spoke in your first letter of seeing a young girl swinging in a hammock under your chamber window, I was somehow strangely drawn to her. I cannot account for it in the least. What you have subsequently written of Miss Daw has strengthened the impression. You seem to be describing a woman I have known in some previous state of existence, or dreamed of in this. Upon my word, if you were to send me her photograph, I believe I should recognize her at a glance. Her manner, that listening attitude, her traits of character, as you indicate them, the light hair and the dark eyes,—they are all familiar things to me. Asked a lot of questions, did she? Curious about me? That is strange.

You would laugh in your sleeve, you wretched old cynic, if you knew how I lie awake nights, with my gas turned down to a star, thinking of The Pines and the house across the road. How cool it must be down there! I long for the salt smell in the air. I picture the colonel smoking his cheroot on the piazza. I send you and Miss Daw off on afternoon rambles along the beach. Sometimes I let you stroll with her under the elms in the moonlight, for you are great friends by this time, I take it, and see each other every day. I know your ways and your manners! Then I fall into a truculent mood, and would like to destroy somebody. Have you noticed anything in the shape of a lover hanging around the colonial Lares and Penates?[14] Does that lieutenant of the horse-marines or that young Stillwater parson visit the house much? Not that I am pining for news of them, but any gossip of the kind would be in order. I wonder, Ned, you don't fall in love with Miss Daw. I am ripe to do it myself. Speaking of photographs, could n't you manage to slip one of her *cartes-de-visite* from her album,—she must have an album, you know,—and send it to me? I will return it before it could be missed. That's a good fellow! Did the mare arrive safe and sound? It will be a capital animal this autumn for Central Park.

O—my leg? I forgot about my leg. It's better.

## VII. Edward Delaney to John Flemming.

August 20,—.

You are correct in your surmises. I am on the most friendly terms with our neighbors. The colonel and my father smoke their afternoon cigar together in our sitting-room or on the piazza opposite, and I pass an hour or two of the day or the evening with the daughter. I am more and more struck by the beauty, modesty, and intelligence of Miss Daw.

---

[13] **Roederer:** A French producer of fine champagne.
[14] **Lares and Penates:** Household spirits in classical Rome, often represented by small figurines.

You ask me why I do not fall in love with her. I will be frank, Jack: I have thought of that. She is young, rich, accomplished, uniting in herself more attractions, mental and personal, than I can recall in any girl of my acquaintance; but she lacks the something that would be necessary to inspire in me that kind of interest. Possessing this unknown quantity, a woman neither beautiful nor wealthy nor very young could bring me to her feet. But not Miss Daw. If we were shipwrecked together on an uninhabited island,—let me suggest a tropical island, for it costs no more to be picturesque,—I would build her a bamboo hut, I would fetch her bread-fruit and cocoanuts, I would fry yams for her, I would lure the ingenuous turtle and make her nourishing soups, but I would n't make love to her,—not under eighteen months. I would like to have her for a sister, that I might shield her and counsel her, and spend half my income on threadlaces and camel's-hair shawls. (We are off the island now.) If such were not my feeling, there would still be an obstacle to my loving Miss Daw. A greater misfortune could scarcely befall me than to love her. Flemming, I am about to make a revelation that will astonish you. I may be all wrong in my premises and consequently in my conclusions; but you shall judge.

That night when I returned to my room after the croquet party at the Daws', and was thinking over the trivial events of the evening, I was suddenly impressed by the air of eager attention with which Miss Daw had followed my account of your accident. I think I mentioned this to you. Well, the next morning, as I went to mail my letter, I overtook Miss Daw on the road to Rye, where the post-office is, and accompanied her thither and back, an hour's walk. The conversation again turned on you, and again I remarked that inexplicable look of interest which had lighted up her face the previous evening. Since then, I have seen Miss Daw perhaps ten times, perhaps oftener, and on each occasion I found that when I was not speaking of you, or your sister, or some person or place associated with you, I was not holding her attention. She would be absent-minded, her eyes would wander away from me to the sea, or to some distant object in the landscape; her fingers would play with the leaves of a book in a way that convinced me she was not listening. At these moments if I abruptly changed the theme,—I did it several times as an experiment,—and dropped some remark about my friend Flemming, then the sombre blue eyes would come back to me instantly.

Now, is not this the oddest thing in the world? No, not the oddest. The effect which you tell me was produced on you by my casual mention of an unknown girl swinging in a hammock is certainly as strange. You can conjecture how that passage in your letter of Friday startled me. Is it possible, then, that two people who have never met, and who are hundreds of miles apart, can exert a magnetic influence on each other? I have read of such psychological phenomena, but never credited them. I leave the solution of the problem to you. As for myself, all other things being favorable, it would be impossible for me to fall in love with a woman who listens to me only when I am talking of my friend!

I am not aware that any one is paying marked attention to my fair neighbor. The lieutenant of the navy—he is stationed at Rivermouth—sometimes drops in of an evening, and sometimes the rector from Stillwater; the lieutenant the oftener. He was there last night. I would not be surprised if he had an eye to the heiress; but he is not formidable. Mistress Daw carries a neat little spear of irony, and the honest lieutenant seems to have a particular facility for impaling himself on the point of it. He is not dangerous, I should say; though I have known a woman to satirize a man for years, and marry him after all. Decidedly, the lowly rector is not dangerous; yet, again, who has not seen Cloth of Frieze victorious in the lists where Cloth of Gold went down?

As to the photograph. There is an exquisite ivorytype of Marjorie, in passe-partout, on the drawing-room mantel-piece. It would be missed at once, if taken. I would do anything reasonable for you, Jack; but I've no burning desire to be hauled up before the local justice of the peace, on a charge of petty larceny.

P. S.—Enclosed is a spray of mignonette,[15] which I advise you to treat tenderly. Yes, we talked of you again last night, as usual. It is becoming a little dreary for me.

## VIII. EDWARD DELANEY TO JOHN FLEMMING.

AUGUST 22,—.

YOUR letter in reply to my last has occupied my thoughts all the morning. I do not know what to think. Do you mean to say that you are seriously half in love with a woman whom you have never seen,—with a shadow, a chimera? for what else can Miss Daw be to you? I do not understand it at all. I understand neither you nor her. You are a couple of ethereal beings moving in finer air than I can breathe with my commonplace lungs. Such delicacy of sentiment is something I admire without comprehending. I am bewildered. I am of the earth earthy, and I find myself in the incongruous position of having to do with mere souls, with natures so finely tempered that I run some risk of shattering them in my awkwardness. I am as Caliban[16] among the spirits!

Reflecting on your letter, I am not sure it is wise in me to continue this correspondence. But no, Jack; I do wrong to doubt the good sense that forms the basis of your character. You are deeply interested in Miss Daw; you feel that she is a person whom you may perhaps greatly admire when you know her: at the same time you bear in mind that the chances are ten to five that, when you do come to know her, she will fall far short of your ideal, and you will not care for her in the least. Look at it in this sensible light, and I will hold back nothing from you.

Yesterday afternoon my father and myself rode over to Rivermouth with the Daws. A heavy rain in the morning had cooled the atmosphere and laid the dust. To Rivermouth is a drive of eight miles, along a winding road lined all the way with wild barberry-bushes. I never saw anything more brilliant than these bushes, the green of the foliage and the pink of the coral berries intensified by the rain. The colonel

---

[15] **mignonette:** A fragrant flower used in potpourri and perfumes; in Roman times, it was used as a balm to heal bruises and as a sedative.
[16] **Caliban:** The brutish and wild man in Shakespeare's *Tempest*.

drove, with my father in front, Miss Daw and I on the back seat. I resolved that for the first five miles your name should not pass my lips. I was amused by the artful attempts she made, at the start, to break through my reticence. Then a silence fell upon her; and then she became suddenly gay. That keenness which I enjoyed so much when it was exercised on the lieutenant was not so satisfactory directed against myself. Miss Daw has great sweetness of disposition, but she can be disagreeable. She is like the young lady in the rhyme, with the curl on her forehead,

> "When she is good,
>     She is very, very good,
> And when she is bad, she is horrid!"

I kept to my resolution, however; but on the return home I relented, and talked of your mare! Miss Daw is going to try a side-saddle on Margot some morning. The animal is a trifle too light for my weight. By the by, I nearly forgot to say Miss Daw sat for a picture yesterday to a Rivermouth artist. If the negative turns out well, I am to have a copy. So our ends will be accomplished without crime. I wish, though, I could send you the ivorytype in the drawing-room; it is cleverly colored, and would give you an idea of her hair and eyes, which of course the other will not.

No, Jack, the spray of mignonette did not come from me. A man of twenty-eight does n't enclose flowers in his letters—to another man. But don't attach too much significance to the circumstance. She gives sprays of mignonette to the rector, sprays to the lieutenant. She has even given a rose from her bosom to your slave. It is her jocund nature to scatter flowers, like Spring.

If my letters sometimes read disjointedly, you must understand that I never finish one at a sitting, but write at intervals, when the mood is on me.

The mood is not on me now.

## IX. EDWARD DELANEY TO JOHN FLEMMING.

AUGUST 23,—.

I HAVE just returned from the strangest interview with Marjorie. She has all but confessed to me her interest in you. But with what modesty and dignity! Her words elude my pen as I attempt to put them on paper; and, indeed, it was not so much what she said as her manner; and that I cannot reproduce. Perhaps it was of a piece with the strangeness of this whole business, that she should tacitly acknowledge to a third party the love she feels for a man she has never beheld! But I have lost, through your aid, the faculty of being surprised. I accept things as people do in dreams. Now that I am again in my room, it all appears like an illusion,—the black masses of Rembrandtish shadow under the trees, the fire-flies whirling in Pyrrhic dances among the shrubbery, the sea over there, Marjorie sitting on the hammock!

It is past midnight, and I am too sleepy to write more.

THURSDAY MORNING.

My father has suddenly taken it into his head to spend a few days at the Shoals. In the mean while you will not hear from me. I see Marjorie walking in the garden with the colonel. I wish I could speak to her alone, but shall probably not have an opportunity before we leave.

## X. EDWARD DELANEY TO JOHN FLEMMING.

AUGUST 28,—.

YOU were passing into your second childhood, were you? Your intellect was so reduced that my epistolary gifts seemed quite considerable to you, did they? I rise superior to the sarcasm in your favor of the 11th instant, when I notice that five days' silence on my part is sufficient to throw you into the depths of despondency.

We returned only this morning from Appledore, that enchanted island,—at four dollars per day. I find on my desk three letters from you! Evidently there is no lingering doubt in *your* mind as to the pleasure I derive from your correspondence. These letters are undated, but in what I take to be the latest are two passages that require my consideration. You will pardon my candor, dear Flemming, but the conviction forces itself upon me that as your leg grows stronger your head becomes weaker. You ask my advice on a certain point. I will give it. In my opinion you could do nothing more unwise than to address a note to Miss Daw, thanking her for the flower. It would, I am sure, offend her delicacy beyond pardon. She knows you only through me; you are to her an abstraction, a figure in a dream,— a dream from which the faintest shock would awaken her. Of course, if you enclose a note to me and insist on its delivery, I shall deliver it; but I advise you not to do so.

You say you are able, with the aid of a cane, to walk about your chamber, and that you purpose to come to The Pines the instant Dillon thinks you strong enough to stand the journey. Again I advise you not to. Do you not see that, every hour you remain away, Marjorie's glamour deepens, and your influence over her increases? You will ruin everything by precipitancy. Wait until you are entirely recovered; in any case, do not come without giving me warning. I fear the effect of your abrupt advent here—under the circumstances.

Miss Daw was evidently glad to see us back again, and gave me both hands in the frankest way. She stopped at the door a moment, this afternoon, in the carriage; she had been over to Rivermouth for her pictures. Unluckily the photographer had spilt some acid on the plate, and she was obliged to give him another sitting. I have an intuition that something is troubling Marjorie. She had an abstracted air not usual with her. However, it may be only my fancy…. I end this, leaving several things unsaid, to accompany my father on one of those long walks which are now his chief medicine,—and mine!

## XI. Edward Delaney to John Flemming.

August 29,—.

I write in great haste to tell you what has taken place here since my letter of last night. I am in the utmost perplexity. Only one thing is plain,—*you* must not dream of coming to The Pines. Marjorie has told her father everything! I saw her for a few minutes, an hour ago, in the garden; and, as near as I could gather from her confused statement, the facts are these: Lieutenant Bradly—that's the naval officer stationed at Rivermouth—has been paying court to Miss Daw for some time past, but not so much to her liking as to that of the colonel, who it seems is an old friend of the young gentleman's father. Yesterday (I knew she was in some trouble when she drove up to our gate) the colonel spoke to Marjorie of Bradly,—urged his suit, I infer. Marjorie expressed her dislike for the lieutenant with characteristic frankness, and finally confessed to her father—well, I really do not know what she confessed. It must have been the vaguest of confessions, and must have sufficiently puzzled the colonel. At any rate; it exasperated him. I suppose I am implicated in the matter, and that the colonel feels bitterly towards me. I do not see why: I have carried no messages between you and Miss Daw; I have behaved with the greatest discretion. I can find no flaw anywhere in my proceeding. I do not see that anybody has done anything,—except the colonel himself.

It is probable, nevertheless, that the friendly relations between the two houses will be broken off. "A plague o' both your houses," say you. I will keep you informed, as well as I can, of what occurs over the way. We shall remain here until the second week in September. Stay where you are, or, at all events, do not dream of joining me…. Colonel Daw is sitting on the piazza looking rather wicked. I have not seen Marjorie since I parted with her in the garden.

## XII. Edward Delaney to Thomas Dillon, M. D., Madison Square, New York.

August 30,—.

My dear Doctor: If you have any influence over Flemming, I beg of you to exert it to prevent his coming to this place at present. There are circumstances, which I will explain to you before long, that make it of the first importance that he should not come into this neighborhood. His appearance here, I speak advisedly, would be disastrous to him. In urging him to remain in New York, or to go to some inland resort, you will be doing him and me a real service. Of course you will not mention my name in this connection. You know me well enough, my dear doctor, to be assured that, in begging your secret co-operation, I have reasons that will meet your entire approval when they are made plain to you. We shall return to town on the 15th of next month, and my first duty will be to present myself at your hospitable door and satisfy your curiosity, if I have excited it. My father, I am glad to state, has so greatly improved that he can no longer be regarded as an invalid. With great esteem, I am, etc., etc.

## XIII. Edward Delaney to John Flemming.

August 31,—.

Your letter, announcing your mad determination to come here, has just reached me. I beseech you to reflect a moment. The step would be fatal to your interests and hers. You would furnish just cause for irritation to R. W. D.; and, though he loves Marjorie tenderly, he is capable of going to any lengths if opposed. You would not like, I am convinced, to be the means of causing him to treat *her* with severity. That would be the result of your presence at The Pines at this juncture. I am annoyed to be obliged to point out these things to you. We are on very delicate ground, Jack; the situation is critical, and the slightest mistake in a move would cost us the game. If you consider it worth the winning, be patient. Trust a little to my sagacity. Wait and see what happens. Moreover, I understand from Dillon that you are in no condition to take so long a journey. He thinks the air of the coast would be the worst thing possible for you; that you ought to go inland, if anywhere. Be advised by me. Be advised by Dillon.

## XIV. Telegrams.

September 1,—.

1.—To Edward Delaney.
Letter received. Dillon be hanged. I think I ought to be on the ground.

J. F.

2.—To John Flemming.
Stay where you are. You would only complicate matters. Do not move until you hear from me.

E. D.

3.—To Edward Delaney.
My being at The Pines could be kept secret. I must see her.

J. F.

4.—To John Flemming.
Do not think of it. It would be useless. R. W. D. has locked M. in her room. You would not be able to effect an interview.

E. D.

5.—To Edward Delaney.
Locked her in her room. Good God. That settles the question. I shall leave by the twelve-fifteen express.

J. F.

## XV. The Arrival.

On the second of September, 187—, as the down express due at 3.40 left the station at Hampton, a young man, leaning on the shoulder of a servant, whom he addressed as Watkins, stepped from the platform into a hack, and requested to be driven to "The Pines." On arriving at the gate of a modest farm-house, a few miles from the station, the young man descended with difficulty from the carriage, and, casting a hasty glance across the road, seemed much impressed by some peculiarity in the landscape. Again leaning on the shoulder of the person Watkins, he walked to the door of the farm-house and inquired for Mr. Edward Delaney. He was informed by the aged man who answered his knock, that Mr. Edward Delaney had gone to Boston the day before, but that Mr. Jonas Delaney was within. This information did not appear satisfactory to the stranger, who inquired if Mr. Edward Delaney had left any message for Mr. John Flemming. There *was* a letter for Mr. Flemming, if he were that person. After a brief absence the aged man reappeared with a Letter.

## XVI. Edward Delaney to John Flemming.

SEPTEMBER 1,—.

I am horror-stricken at what I have done ! When I began this correspondence I had no other purpose than to relieve the tedium of your sick-chamber. Dillon told me to cheer you up. I tried to. I thought you entered into the spirit of the thing. I had no idea, until within a few days, that you were taking matters *au sérieux*.

What can I say? I am in sackcloth and ashes. I am a pariah, a dog of an outcast. I tried to make a little romance to interest you, something soothing and idyllic, and, by Jove! I have done it only too well! My father does n't know a word of this, so don't jar the old gentleman any more than you can help. I fly from the wrath to come—when you arrive! For O, dear Jack, there is n't any colonial mansion on the other side of the road, there is n't any piazza, there is n't any hammock,—there is n't any Marjorie Daw!!

—1873

## Constance Fenimore Woolson 1840–1894

Constance Fenimore Woolson has always had admirers of her fiction, but she is difficult to pin down. She produced books of short fiction about the lake country of Michigan and about the South, but she is not fundamentally a local color writer, particularly if that label implies nostalgia and a reverence for a specific place. She also produced a great deal of fiction set in Europe, especially Italy, but her sense of American expatriate experience abroad differs sharply from that of her friend and admirer, Henry James, even though both share a fascination with the fate of artists in unreceptive communities. She certainly had a keen eye for the details of a particular place, but perhaps the distinguishing quality of her fiction is her subtle form of psychological realism. Her best fiction often focuses on forms of obsession—sometimes with a place, sometimes with a person, and sometimes with an idea or ambition. She renders the details of external life with a fidelity to the psychological truth those details reveal.

"The Lady of Little Fishing" is one of the strongest stories from her first book, *Castle Nowhere: Lake Country Sketches* (1875). In many ways, it is clearly a revision of one of Bret Harte's most famous stories, "The Luck of Roaring Camp," but it is a revision with a vengeance. Woolson's focus is on the ways in which men construct women into objects of fantasy that meet their own emotional needs while ignoring the reality embodied in every complex human being. It is thus a remarkable study in gender roles and a counterpart to the other stories in this thematic section.

**Further Reading** Sharon Dean, *Constance Fenimore Woolson: Homeward Bound* (1995); Rayburn S. Moore, *Constance F. Woolson* (1963); Cheryl B. Torsney, *Constance Fenimore Woolson: The Grief of Artistry* (1989).

# The Lady of Little Fishing

IT was an island in Lake Superior.

I beached my canoe there about four o'clock in the afternoon, for the wind was against me, and a high sea running. The late summer of 1850, and I was coasting along the south shore of the great lake, hunting, fishing, and camping on the beach, under the delusion that in that way I was living "close to the great heart of nature,"—whatever that may mean. Lord Bacon got up the phrase; I suppose he knew. Pulling the boat high and dry on the sand with the comfortable reflection that here were no tides to disturb her with their goings-out and comings-in, I strolled through the woods on a tour of exploration, expecting to find the blue-bells, Indian pipes, juniper rings, perhaps a few agates along shore, possibly a bird or two for company. I found a town.

It was deserted; but none the less a town, with three streets, residences, a meeting-house, gardens, a little park, and an attempt at a fountain. Ruins are rare in the New World; I took off my hat. "Hail, homes of the past!" I said. (I cultivated the habit of thinking aloud when I was living close to the great heart of nature.) "A human voice resounds through your arches" (there were no arches,—logs won't arch; but never mind) "once more, a human hand touches your venerable walls, a human foot presses your deserted hearth-stones." I then selected the best half of the meeting-house for my camp, knocked down one of the homes for fuel, and kindled a glorious bonfire in the park. "Now that you are illuminated with joy, O Ruin," I remarked, "I will go down to the beach and bring up my supplies. It is long since I have had a roof over my head; I promise you to stay until your last residence is well burned; then I will make a final cup of coffee with the meeting-house itself, and depart in peace, leaving your poor old bones buried in decent ashes."

The ruin made no objection, and I took up my abode there; the roof of the meeting-house was still water-tight (which is an advantage when the great heart of nature grows wet). I kindled a fire on the sacerdotal hearth, cooked my supper, ate it in leisurely comfort, and then stretched myself on a blanket to enjoy an evening pipe of peace, listening meanwhile to the sounding of the wind through the great pine-trees. There was no door to my sanctuary, but I had the cozy far end; the island was uninhabited, there was not a boat in sight at sunset, nothing could disturb me unless it might be a ghost. Presently a ghost came in.

It did not wear the traditional gray tarlatan armor of Hamlet's father, the only ghost with whom I am well acquainted; this spectre was clad in substantial deer-skin garments, and carried a gun and loaded game-bag. It came forward to my hearth, hung up its gun, opened its game-bag, took out some birds, and inspected them gravely.

"Fat?" I inquired.

"They'll do," replied the spectre, and forthwith set to work preparing them for the coals. I smoked on in silence. The spectre seemed to be a skilled cook, and after deftly broiling its supper, it offered me a share; I accepted. It swallowed a huge mouthful and crunched with its teeth; the spell was broken, and I knew it for a man of flesh and blood.

He gave his name as Reuben, and proved himself an excellent camping companion; in fact, he shot all the game, caught all the fish, made all the fires, and cooked all the food for us both. I proposed to him to stay and help me burn up the ruin, with the condition that when the last timber of the meeting-house was consumed, we should shake hands and depart, one to the east, one to the west, without a backward glance. "In that way we shall not infringe upon each other's personality," I said.

"Agreed," replied Reuben.

He was a man of between fifty and sixty years, while I was on the sunny side of thirty; he was reserved, I was always generously affable; he was an excellent cook, while I—well, I was n't; he was taciturn, and so, in payment for the work he did, I entertained him with conversation, or rather monologue, in my most brilliant style. It took only two weeks to burn up the town, burned we never so slowly; at last it came the turn of the meeting-house, which now stood by itself in the vacant clearing. It was a cool September day; we cooked breakfast with the roof, dinner with the sides, supper with the odds and ends, and then applied a torch to the frame-work. Our last camp-fire was a glorious one. We lay stretched on our blankets, smoking and watching the glow. "I wonder, now, who built the old shanty," I said in a musing tone.

"Well," replied Reuben, slowly, "if you really want to know, I will tell you. I did."

"You!"

"Yes."

"You did n't do it alone?"

"No; there were about forty of us."

"Here?"

"Yes; here at Little Fishing."

"Little Fishing?"

"Yes; Little Fishing Island. That is the name of the place."

"How long ago was this?"

"Thirty years."

"Hunting and trapping, I suppose?"

"Yes; for the Northwest and Hudson Bay companies."

"Was n't a meeting-house an unusual accompaniment?"

"Most unusual."

"Accounted for in this case by"—

"A woman."

"Ah!" I said in a tone of relish; "then of course there is a story?"

"There is."

"Out with it, comrade. I scarcely expected to find the woman and her story up here; but since the irrepressible creature would come, out with her by all means. She shall grace our last pipe together, the last timber of our meeting-house, our last night on Little Fishing. The dawn will see us far from each other, to meet no more this side heaven. Speak then, O comrade mine! I am in one of my rare listening moods!"

I stretched myself at ease and waited. Reuben was a long time beginning, but I was too indolent to urge him. At length he spoke.

"They were a rough set here at Little Fishing, all the worse for being all white men; most of the other camps were full of half-breeds and Indians. The island had been a station away back in the early days of the Hudson Bay Company; it was a station for the Northwest Company while that lasted; then it went back to the Hudson, and stayed there until the company moved its forces farther to the north. It was not at any time a regular post; only a camp for the hunters. The post was farther down the lake. Oh, but those were wild days! You think you know the wilderness, boy; but you know nothing, absolutely nothing. It makes me laugh to see the airs of you city gentlemen with your fine guns, improved fishing-tackle, elaborate paraphernalia, as though you were going to wed the whole forest, floating up and down the lake for a month or two in the summer! You should have seen the hunters of Little Fishing going out gayly when the mercury was down twenty degrees below zero, for a week in the woods. You should have seen the trappers wading through the hard snow, breast high, in the gray dawn, visiting the traps and hauling home the prey. There were all kinds of men here, Scotch, French, English, and American; all classes, the high and the low, the educated and the ignorant; all sorts, the lazy and the hard-working. One thing only they all had in common—badness. Some had fled to the wilderness to escape the law, others to escape order; some had chosen the wild life because of its wildness, others had drifted into it from sheer lethargy. This far northern border did not attract the plodding emigrant, the respectable settler. Little

Fishing held none of that trash; only a reckless set of fellows who carried their lives in their hands, and tossed them up, if need be, without a second thought."

"And other people's lives without a third," I suggested.

"Yes; if they deserved it. But nobody whined; there was n't any nonsense here. The men went hunting and trapping, got the furs ready for the bateaux, ate when they were hungry, drank when they were thirsty, slept when they were sleepy, played cards when they felt like it, and got angry and knocked each other down whenever they chose. As I said before, there wasn't any nonsense at Little Fishing,—until *she* came."

"Ah! the she!"

"Yes, the Lady,—our Lady, as we called her. Thirty-one years ago; how long it seems!"

"And well it may," I said. "Why, comrade, I was n't born then!"

This stupendous fact seemed to strike me more than my companion; he went on with his story as though I had not spoken.

"One October evening, four of the boys had got into a row over the cards; the rest of us had come out of our wigwams to see the fun, and were sitting around on the stumps, chaffing them, and laughing; the camp-fire was burning in front, lighting up the woods with a red glow for a short distance, and making the rest doubly black all around. There we all were, as I said before, quite easy and comfortable, when suddenly there appeared among us, as though she had dropped from heaven, a woman!

"She was tall and slender, the firelight shone full on her pale face and dove-colored dress, her golden hair was folded back under a little white cap, and a white kerchief lay over her shoulders; she looked spotless. I stared; I could scarcely believe my eyes; none of us could. There was not a white woman west of the Sault Ste. Marie. The four fellows at the table sat as if transfixed; one had his partner by the throat, the other two were disputing over a point in the game. The lily lady glided up to their table, gathered the cards in her white hands, slowly, steadily, without pause or trepidation before their astonished eyes, and then, coming back, she threw the cards into the centre of the glowing fire. 'Ye shall not play away your souls,' she said in a clear, sweet voice. 'Is not the game sin? And its reward death?' And then, immediately, she gave us a sermon, the like of which was never heard before; no argument, no doctrine, just simple, pure entreaty. 'For the love of God,' she ended, stretching out her hands towards our silent, gazing group, 'for the love of God, my brothers, try to do better.'

"We did try; but it was not for the love of God. Neither did any of us feel like brothers.

"She did not give any name; we called her simply our Lady, and she accepted the title. A bundle carefully packed in birch-bark was found on the beach. 'Is this yours?' asked Black Andy.

" 'It is,' replied the Lady; and removing his hat, the black-haired giant carried the package reverently inside her lodge. For we had given her our best wigwam, and fenced it off with pine saplings so that it looked like a miniature fortress. The Lady did not suggest this stockade; it was our own idea, and with one accord we worked at it like beavers, and hung up a gate with a ponderous bolt inside.

"'Mais, ze can nevare farsen eet wiz her leetle fingares,' said Frenchy, a sallow little wretch with a turn for handicraft; so he contrived a small spring which shot the bolt into place with a touch. The Lady lived in her fortress; three times a day the men carried food to her door, and, after tapping gently, withdrew again, stumbling over each other in their haste. The Flying Dutchman, a stolid Holland-born sailor, was our best cook, and the pans and kettles were generally left to him; but now all wanted to try their skill, and the results were extraordinary.

"'She's never touched that pudding, now,' said Nightingale Jack, discontentedly, as his concoction of berries and paste came back from the fortress door.

"'She will starve soon, I think,' remarked the Doctor, calmly; 'to my certain knowledge she has not had an eatable meal for four days.' And he lighted a fresh pipe. This was an aside, and the men pretended not to hear it; but the pans were relinquished to the Dutchman from that time forth.

"The Lady wore always her dove-colored robe, and little white cap, through whose muslin we could see the glimmer of her golden hair. She came and went among us like a spirit; she knew no fear; she turned our life inside out, nor shrank from its vileness. It seemed as though she was not of earth, so utterly impersonal was her interest in us, so heavenly her pity. She took up our sins, one by one, as an angel might; she pleaded with us for our own lost souls, she spared us not, she held not back one grain of denunciation, one iota of future punishment. Sometimes, for days, we would not see her; then, at twilight, she would glide out among us, and, standing in the light of the camp-fire, she would preach to us as though inspired. We listened to her; I do not mean that we were one whit better at heart, but still we listened to her, always. It was a wonderful sight that lily face under the pine-trees, that spotless woman standing alone in the glare of the fire, while around her lay forty evil-minded, lawless men, not one of whom but would have killed his neighbor for so much as a disrespectful thought of her.

"So strange was her coming, so almost supernatural her appearance in this far forest, that we never wondered over its cause, but simply accepted it as a sort of miracle; your thoroughly irreligious men are always superstitious. Not one of us would have asked a question, and we should never have known her story had she not herself told it to us; not immediately, not as though it was of any importance, but quietly, briefly, and candidly as a child. She came, she said, from Scotland, with a band of God's people. She had always been in one house, a religious institution of some kind, sewing for the poor when her strength allowed it, but generally ill, and suffering much from pain in her head; often kept under the influence of soothing medicines for days together. She had no father or mother. she was only one of this band; and when they decided to send out missionaries to America, she begged to go, although but a burden; the sea voyage restored her health; she grew, she said, in strength and in grace, and her heart was as the heart of a lion. Word came to her from on high that she should come up into the northern lake-country and preach the gospel there; the band were going to the verdant prairies. She left them in the night, taking nothing but her clothing; a friendly vessel carried her north; she had preached the gospel everywhere. At the Sault the priests had driven her out, but nothing fearing, she went on into the wilderness, and so, coming part of the way in canoes, part of the way along shore, she had reached our far island. Marvelous kindness had she met with, she said; the Indians, the half-breeds, the hunters, and the trappers, had all received her, and helped her on her way from camp to camp. They had listened to her words also. At Portage they had begged her to stay through the winter, and offered to build her a little church for Sunday services. Our men looked at each other. Portage was the worst camp on the lake, notorious for its fights; it was a mining settlement.

" 'But I told them I must journey on towards the west,' continued our Lady. 'I am called to visit every camp on this shore before the winter sets in; I must soon leave you also.'

"The men looked at each other again; the Doctor was spokesman. 'But, my Lady,' he said, 'the next post is Fort William, two hundred and thirty-five miles away on the north shore.'

" 'It is almost November; the snow will soon be six and ten feet deep. The Lady could never travel through it—could she, now?' said Black Andy, who had begun eagerly, but in his embarrassment at the sound of his own voice, now turned to Frenchy and kicked him covertly into answering.

" 'Nevare!' replied the Frenchman; he had intended to place his hand upon his heart to give emphasis to his word, but the Lady turned her calm eyes that way, and his grimy paw fell, its gallantry wilted.

" 'I thought there was one more camp,—at Burnt-Wood River,' said our Lady in a musing tone. The men looked at each other a third time; there was a camp there, and they all knew it. But the Doctor was equal to the emergency.

" 'That camp, my Lady,' he said gravely, 'that camp no longer exists!' Then he whispered hurriedly to the rest of us, 'It will be an easy job to clean it out, boys. We'll send over a party to-night; it's only thirty-five miles.'

"We recognized superior genius; the Doctor was our oldest and deepest sinner. But what struck us most was his anxiety to make good his lie. Had it then come to this,—that the Doctor told the truth?

"The next day we all went to work to build our Lady a church; in a week it was completed. There goes its last cross-beam now into the fire; it was a solid piece of work, was n't it? It has stood this climate thirty years. I remember the first Sunday service; we all washed, and dressed ourselves in the best we had; we scarcely knew each other, we were so fine. The Lady was pleased with the church, but yet she had not said she would stay all winter; we were still anxious. How she preached to us that day! We had made a screen of young spruces set in boxes, and her figure stood out against the dark green background like a thing of light. Her silvery voice rang through the log temple, her face seemed to us like a star. She had no color in her cheeks at any time; her dress, too, was colorless. Although gentle, there was an iron inflexibility about her slight, erect form. We felt, as we saw her standing there, that if need be she would walk up to the lion's jaws, the cannon's mouth, with a smile. She took a little book from her pocket and read to us a hymn: 'Oh come, all ye faithful,' the old 'Adeste Fideles.' Some of us knew it; she sang, and gradually, shamefacedly, voices joined in. It was a sight to see Nightingale Jack solemnly singing away about 'choirs of angels;' but it was a treat to hear him, too,—what a voice he had! Then our Lady prayed, kneeling down on the little platform in front of the evergreens, clasping her hands, and lifting her eyes to heaven. We did not know what to do at first, but the Doctor gave us a severe look and bent his head, and we all followed his lead.

"When service was over and the door opened, we found that it had been snowing; we could not see out through the windows because white cloth was nailed over them in place of glass.

" 'Now, my Lady, you will have to stay with us,' said the Doctor. We all gathered around with eager faces.

" 'Do you really believe that it will be for the good of your souls?' asked the sweet voice.

"The Doctor believed—for us all.

" 'Do you really hope?'

"The Doctor hoped.

" 'Will you try to do your best?'

"The Doctor was sure he would.

" 'I will,' answered the Flying Dutchman earnestly. 'I moost not fry de meat any more; I moost broil!'

"For we had begged him for months to broil, and he had obstinately refused; broil represented the good, and fry the evil, to his mind; he came out for the good according to his light; but none the less did we fall upon him behind the Lady's back, and cuff him into silence.

"She stayed with us all winter. You don't know what the winters are up here; steady, bitter cold for seven months, thermometer always below, the snow dry as dust, the air like a knife. We built a compact chimney for our Lady, and we cut cords of wood into small, light sticks, easy for her to lift, and stacked them in her shed; we lined her lodge with skins, and we made oil from bear's fat and rigged up a kind of lamp for her. We tried to make candles, I remember, but they would not run straight; they came out hump-backed and sidling, and burned themselves to wick in no time. Then we took to improving the town. We had lived in all kinds of huts and lean-to shanties; now nothing would do but regular log-houses. If it had been summer, I don't know what we might not have run to in the way of piazzas and fancy steps; but with the snow five feet deep, all we could accomplish was a plain, square log-house, and even that took our whole force. The only way to keep the peace was to have all the houses exactly alike; we laid out the three streets, and built the houses, all facing the meeting-house, just as you found them."

"And where was the Lady's lodge?" I asked, for I recalled no stockaded fortress, large or small.

My companion hesitated a moment. Then he said abruptly, "It was torn down."

"Torn down!" I repeated. "Why, what"—

Reuben waved his hand with a gesture that silenced me, and went on with his story. It came to me then for the first time, that he was pursuing the current of his own thoughts rather than entertaining me. I turned to look at him with a new interest. I had talked to him for two weeks, in rather a patronizing way; could it be that affairs were now, at this last moment, reversed?

"It took us almost all winter to build those houses," pursued Reuben. "At one time we neglected the hunting and trapping to such a degree, that the Doctor called a meeting and expressed his opinion. Ours was a voluntary camp, in a measure, but still we had formally agreed to get a certain amount of skins ready for the bateaux[1] by early spring; this agreement was about the only real bond of union between us. Those whose houses were not completed scowled at the Doctor.

"'Do you suppose I'm going to live like an Injun when the other fellows has regular houses?' inquired Black Andy with a menacing air.

"'By no means,' replied the Doctor, blandly. 'My plan is this: build at night.'

"'At night?'

"'Yes; by the light of pine fires.'

"We did. After that, we faithfully went out hunting and trapping as long as daylight lasted, and then, after supper, we built up huge fires of pine logs, and went to work on the next house. It was a strange picture: the forest deep in snow, black with night, the red glow of the great fires, and our moving figures working on as complacently as though daylight, balmy air, and the best of tools, were ours.

"The Lady liked our industry. She said our new houses showed that the 'new cleanliness of our inner man required a cleaner tabernacle for the outer.' I don't know about our inner man, but our outer was certainly much cleaner.

"One day the Flying Dutchman made one of his unfortunate remarks. 'De boys t'inks you'll like dem better in nize houses,' he announced when, happening to pass the fortress, he found the Lady standing at her gate gazing at the work of the preceding night. Several of the men were near enough to hear him, but too far off to kick him into silence as usual; but they glared at him instead. The Lady looked at the speaker with her dreamy, far-off eyes.

"'De boys t'inks you like dem,' began the Dutchman again, thinking she did not comprehend; but at that instant he caught the combined glare of the six eyes, and stopped abruptly, not at all knowing what was wrong, but sure there was something.

"'Like them,' repeated the Lady dreamily; 'yea, I do like them. Nay, more, I love them. Their souls are as dear to me as the souls of brothers.'

"'Say, Frenchy, have you got a sister?' said Nightingale Jack confidentially, that evening.

---

[1] **bateaux:** *The* French word for "boats"; in this case, it refers to the boats that are to pick up the furs from the trappers.

" 'Mais oui,' said Frenchy.

" 'You think all creation of her, I suppose?'

" 'We fight like four cats and one dog; *she* is the cats,' said the Frenchman concisely.

" 'You don't say so!' replied Jack. 'Now, I never had a sister,—but I thought perhaps'—He paused, and the sentence remained unfinished.

"The Nightingale and I were house-mates. We sat late over our fire not long after that; I gave a gigantic yawn. 'This lifting logs half the night is enough to kill one,' I said, getting out my jug. 'Sing something, Jack. It's a long time since I've heard anything but hymns.'

"Jack always went off as easily as a music-box: you had only to wind him up; the jug was the key. I soon had him in full blast. He was giving out

'The minute gun at sea—the minute gun at sea,'

with all the pathos of his tenor voice, when the door burst open and the whole population rushed in upon us.

" 'What do you mean by shouting this way, in the middle of the night?'

" 'Shut up your howling, Jack.'

" 'How do you suppose any one can sleep?'

" 'It's a disgrace to the camp!'

" 'Now then, gentlemen,' I replied, for my blood was up (whisky, perhaps), 'is this my house, or is n't it? If I want music, I'll have it. Time was when you were not so particular.'

"It was the first word of rebellion. The men looked at each other, then at me.

" 'I'll go and ask her if she objects,' I continued boldly.

" 'No, no. You shall not.'

" 'Let him go,' said the Doctor, who stood smoking his pipe on the outskirts of the crowd. 'It is just as well to have that point settled now. The Minute Gun at Sea is a good moral song in its way,—a sort of marine missionary affair.'

"So I started, the others followed; we all knew that the Lady watched late; we often saw the glimmer of her lamp far on towards morning. It was burning now. The gate was fastened, I knocked; no answer. I knocked again, and yet a third time; still, silence. The men stood off at a little distance and waited. 'She shall answer,' I said angrily, and going around to the side where the stockade came nearer to the wall of the lodge, I knocked loudly on the close-set saplings. For answer I thought I heard a low moan; I listened, it came again. My anger vanished, and with a mighty bound I swung myself up to the top of the stockade, sprung down inside, ran around, and tried the door. It was fastened; I burst it open and entered. There, by the light of the hanging lamp, I saw the Lady on the floor, apparently dead. I raised her in my arms; her heart was beating faintly, but she was unconscious. I had seen many fainting fits; this was something different; the limbs were rigid. I laid her on the low couch, loosened her dress, bathed her head and face in cold water, and wrenched up one of the warm hearth-stones to apply to her feet. I did not hesitate; I saw that it was a dangerous case, something like a trance or an 'ecstasis.' Somebody must attend to her, and there were only men to choose from. Then why not I?

"I heard the others talking outside; they could not understand the delay; but I never heeded, and kept on my work. To tell the truth, I had studied medicine, and felt a genuine enthusiasm over a rare case. Once my patient opened her eyes and looked at me, then she lapsed away again into unconsciousness in spite of all my efforts. At last the men outside came in, angry and suspicious; they had broken down the gate. There we all stood, the whole forty of us, around the deathlike form of our Lady.

"What a night it was! To give her air, the men camped outside in the snow with a line of pickets in whispering distance from each other from the bed to their anxious group. Two were detailed to help me—the Doctor (whose title was a sarcastic D. D.) and Jimmy, a gentle little man, excellent at bandaging broken limbs. Every vial in the camp was brought in—astonishing lotions, drops, and balms; each man produced something; they did their best, poor fellows, and wore out the night with their anxiety. At dawn our Lady revived suddenly, thanked us all, and assured us that she felt quite well again; the trance was over. 'It was my old enemy,' she said, 'the old illness of Scotland, which I hoped had left me forever. But I am thankful that it is no worse; I have come out of it with a clear brain. Sing a hymn of thankfulness for me, dear friends, before you go.'

"Now, we sang on Sunday in the church; but then she led us, and we had a kind of an idea that after all she did not hear us. But now, who was to lead us? We stood awkwardly around the bed, and shuffled our hats in our uneasy fingers. The Doctor fixed his eyes upon the Nightingale; Jack saw it and cowered. 'Begin,' said the Doctor in a soft voice; but gripping him in the back at the same time with an ominous clutch.

" 'I don't know the words,' faltered the unhappy Nightingale.

" 'Now thank we all our God,
    With hearts and hands and voices,'

began the Doctor, and repeated Luther's hymn with perfect accuracy from beginning to end. 'What will happen next? The Doctor knows hymns!' we thought in profound astonishment. But the Nightingale had begun, and gradually our singers joined in; I doubt whether the grand old choral was ever sung by such a company before or since. There was never any further question, by the way, about that minute gun at sea; it stayed at sea as far as we were concerned.

"Spring came, the faltering spring of Lake Superior. I won't go into my own story, but such as it was, the spring brought it back to me with new force. I wanted to go,—and yet I did n't. 'Where,' do you ask? To see her, of course—a woman, the most beautiful—well, never mind all that. To be brief, I loved her; she scorned me; I thought I had learned to hate her—but—I was n't sure about it now. I kept myself aloof from the others and gave up my heart to the old sweet, bitter memories; I did not even go to church on Sundays. But all the rest went; our Lady's influence was as great as ever.

I could hear them singing; they sang better now that they could have the door open; the pent-up feeling used to stifle them. The time for the bateaux drew near, and I noticed that several of the men were hard at work packing the furs in bales, a job usually left to the *voyageurs* who came with the boats. 'What's that for?' I asked.

"'You don't suppose we're going to have those bateaux rascals camping on Little Fishing, do you?' said Black Andy scornfully. 'Where are your wits, Reub?'

"And they packed every skin, rafted them all over to the mainland, and waited there patiently for days, until the train of slow boats came along and took off the bales; then they came back in triumph. 'Now we're secure for another six months,' they said, and began to lay out a park, and gardens for every house. The Lady was fond of flowers; the whole town burst into blossom. The Lady liked green grass; all the clearing was soon turfed over like a lawn. The men tried the ice-cold lake every day, waiting anxiously for the time when they could bathe. There was no end to their cleanliness; Black Andy had grown almost white again, and Frenchy's hair shone like oiled silk.

"The Lady stayed on, and all went well. But, gradually, there came a discovery. The Lady was changing—had changed! Gradually, slowly, but none the less distinctly to the eyes that knew her every eyelash. A little more hair was visible over the white brow, there was a faint color in the cheeks, a quicker step; the clear eyes were sometimes downcast now, the steady voice softer, the words at times faltering. In the early summer the white cap vanished, and she stood among us crowned only with her golden hair; one day she was seen through her open door sewing on a white robe! The men noted all these things silently; they were even a little troubled as at something they did not understand, something beyond their reach. Was she planning to leave them?

"'It's my belief she's getting ready to ascend right up into heaven,' said Salem.

"Salem was a little 'wanting,' as it is called, and the men knew it; still, his words made an impression. They watched the Lady with an awe which was almost superstitious; they were troubled and knew not why. But the Lady bloomed on. I did not pay much attention to all this; but I could not help hearing it. My heart was moody, full of its own sorrows; I secluded myself more and more. Gradually I took to going off into the mainland forests for days on solitary hunting expeditions. The camp went on its way rejoicing; the men succeeded, after a world of trouble, in making a fountain which actually played, and they glorified themselves exceedingly. The life grew quite pastoral. There was talk of importing a cow from the East, and a messenger was sent to the Sault for certain choice supplies against the coming winter. But, in the late summer, the whisper went round again that the Lady had changed, this time for the worse. She looked ill, she drooped from day to day; the new life that had come to her vanished, but her former life was not restored. She grew silent and sad, she strayed away by herself through the woods, she scarcely noticed the men who followed her with anxious eyes. Time passed, and brought with it an undercurrent of trouble, suspicion, and anger. Everything went on as before; not one habit, not one custom was altered; both sides seemed to shrink from the first change, however slight. The daily life of the camp was outwardly the same, but brooding trouble filled every heart. There was no open discussion, men talked apart in twos and threes; a gloom rested over everything, but no one said, 'What is the matter?'

"There was a man among us—I have not said much of the individual characters of our party, but this man was one of the least esteemed, or rather liked; there was not much esteem of any kind at Little Fishing. Little was known about him; although the youngest man in the camp, he was a mooning, brooding creature, with brown hair and eyes and a melancholy face. He was n't hearty and whole-souled, and yet he wasn't an out and out rascal; he was n't a leader, and yet he was n't follower either. He would n't be; he was like a third horse, always. There was no goodness about him; don't go to fancying that that was the reason the men did not like him, he was as bad as they were, every inch! He never shirked his work, and they couldn't get a handle on him anywhere; but he was just—unpopular. The why and the wherefore are of no consequence now. Well, do you know what was the suspicion that hovered over the camp? It was this: our Lady loved that man!

"It took three months for all to see it, and yet never a word was spoken. All saw, all heard; but they might have been blind and deaf for any sign they gave. And the Lady drooped more and more.

"September came, the fifteenth; the Lady lay on her couch, pale and thin; the door was open and a bell stood beside her, but there was no line of pickets whispering tidings of her state to an anxious group outside. The turf in the three streets had grown yellow for want of water. the flowers in the little gardens had drooped and died, the fountain was choked with weeds, and the interiors of the houses were all untidy. It was Sunday, and near the hour for service; but the men lounged about, dingy and unwashed.

"'An't you going to church?' said Salem, stopping at the door of one of the houses; he was dressed in his best, with a flower in his button-hole.

"'See him now! See the fool,' said Black Andy. 'He's going to church, he is! And where's the minister, Salem? Answer me that!'

"'Why,—in the church, I suppose,' replied Salem vacantly.

"'No, she an't; not she! She's at home, a-weeping, and a-wailing, and a-gernashing of her teeth,' replied Andy with bitter scorn.

"'What for?' said Salem.

"'What for? Why, that 's the joke! Hear him, boys; he wants to know what for!'

"The loungers laughed,—a loud, reckless laugh.

"'Well, I'm going any way,' said Salem, looking wonderingly from one to the other; he passed on and entered the church.

"'I say, boys, let's have a high old time,' cried Andy savagely. 'Let's go back to the old way and have a jolly Sunday. Let's have out the jugs and the cards and be free again!'

"The men hesitated; ten months and more of law and order held them back.

"'What are you afraid of?' said Andy. 'Not of a canting hypocrite, I hope. She's fooled us long enough, I say. Come on!' He brought out a table and stools, and produced the long unused cards and a jug of whisky. 'Strike up, Jack,' he cried; 'give us old Fiery-Eyes.'

"The Nightingale hesitated. Fiery-Eyes was a rollicking drinking song; but Andy put the glass to his lips and his scruples vanished in the tempting aroma. He began at the top of his voice, partners were chosen, and, trembling with excitement and impatience, like prisoners unexpectedly set free, the men gathered around, and made their bets.

" 'What born fools we've been,' said Black Andy, laying down a card.

" 'Yes,' replied the Flying Dutchman, 'porn fools!' And he followed suit.

"But a thin white hand came down on the bits of colored pasteboard. It was our Lady. With her hair disordered, and the spots of fever in her cheeks, she stood smong us again; but not as of old. Angry eyes confronted her, and Andy wrenched the cards from her grasp. 'No, my Lady,' he said sternly; 'never again!'

"The Lady gazed from one face to the next, and so all around the circle; all were dark and sullen. Then she bowed her head upon her hands and wept aloud.

"There was a sudden shrinking away on all sides, the players rose, the cards were dropped. But the Lady glided away, weeping as she went; she entered the church door and the men could see her taking her accustomed place on the platform. One by one they followed; Black Andy lingered till the last, but he came. The service began, and went on falteringly, without spirit, with palpable fears of a total breaking down which never quite came; the Nightingale sang almost alone, and made sad work with the words; Salem joined in confidently, but did not improve the sense of the hymn. The Lady was silent. But when the time for the sermon came, she rose and her voice burst forth.

" 'Men, brothers, what have I done? A change has come over the town, a change has come over your hearts. You shun me! What have I done?'

"There was a grim silence; then the Doctor rose in his place and answered:

" 'Only this, madam. You have shown yourself to be a woman.'

" 'And what did you think me?'

" 'A saint.'

" 'God forbid!' said the lady, earnestly. 'I never thought myself one.'

" 'I know that well. But you were a saint to us; hence your influence. It is gone.'

" 'Is it all gone?' asked the Lady, sadly.

" 'Yes. Do not deceive yourself; we have never been one whit better save through our love for you. We held you as something high above ourselves; we were content to worship you.'

" 'Oh no, not me!' said the Lady, shuddering.

" 'Yes, you, you alone! But—our idol came down among us and showed herself to be but common flesh and blood! What wonder that we stand aghast? What wonder that our hearts are bitter? What wonder (worse than all!) that when the awe has quite vanished, there is strife for the beautiful image fallen from its niche?'

"The Doctor ceased, and turned away. The Lady stretched out her hands towards the others; her face was deadly pale, and there was a bewildered expression in her eyes.

"'Oh, ye for whom I have prayed, for whom I have struggled to obtain a blessing,—ye whom I have loved so,—do *ye* desert me thus?' she cried.

"'*You* have deserted us,' answered a voice.

"'I have not.'

"'You have,' cried Black Andy, pushing to the front. 'You love that Mitchell! Deny it if you dare!'

"There was an irrepressible murmur, then a sudden hush. The angry suspicion, the numbing certainty had found voice at last; the secret was out. All eyes, which had at first closed with the shock, were now fixed upon the solitary woman before them; they burned like coals.

"'Do I?' murmured the Lady, with a strange questioning look that turned from face to face. 'Do I?—Great God! I do.' She sank upon her knees and buried her face in her trembling hands. 'The truth has come to me at last—I do!'

"Her voice was a mere whisper, but every ear heard it, and every eye saw the crimson rise to the forehead and redden the white throat.

"For a moment there was silence, broken only by the hard breathing of the men. Then the Doctor spoke.

"'Go out and bring him in,' he cried. 'Bring in this Mitchell! It seems he has other things to do,—the blockhead!'

"Two of the men hurried out.

"'He shall not have her,' shouted Black Andy. 'My knife shall see to that!' And he pressed close to the platform. A great tumult arose, men talked angrily and clenched their fists, voices rose and fell together: 'He shall not have her—Mitchell! Mitchell!'

"'The truth is, each one of you wants her himself,' said the Doctor.

"There was a sudden silence, but every man eyed his neighbor jealously; Black Andy stood in front, knife in hand, and kept guard. The Lady had not moved; she was kneeling, with her face buried in her hands.

"'I wish to speak to her,' said the Doctor, advancing.

"'You shall not,' cried Andy, fiercely interposing.

"'You fool! I love her this moment ten thousand times more than you do. But do you suppose I would so much as touch a woman who loved another man?'

"The knife dropped; the Doctor passed on and took his place on the platform by the Lady's side. The tumult began again, for Mitchell was seen coming in the door between his two keepers.

"'Mitchell! Mitchell!' rang angrily through the church.

"'Look, woman!' said the Doctor, bending over the kneeling figure at his side. She raised her head and saw the wolfish faces below.

"'They have had ten months of your religion,' he said.

"It was his revenge. Bitter, indeed; but he loved her.

"In the mean time the man Mitchell was hauled and pushed and tossed forward to the platform by rough hands that longed to throttle him on the way. At last, angry himself, but full of wonder, he confronted them, this crowd of comrades suddenly turned madmen! 'What does this mean?' he asked.

"'Mean! mean!' shouted the men; 'a likely story! He asks what this means!' And they laughed boisterously.

"The Doctor advanced. 'You see this woman,' he said.

"'I see our Lady.'

"'Our Lady no longer; only a woman like any other,—weak and fickle. Take her,—but begone.'

"'Take her!' repeated Mitchell, bewildered. 'Take our Lady! And where?'

"'Fool! Liar! Blockhead!' shouted the crowd below.

"'The truth is simply this, Mitchell,' continued the Doctor, quietly. 'We herewith give you up our Lady,—ours no longer; for she has just confessed, openly confessed, that she loves you.'

"Mitchell started back. 'Loves me!'

"'Yes.'

"Black Andy felt the blade of his knife. 'He'll never have her alive,' he muttered.

"'But,' said Mitchell, bluntly confronting the Doctor, 'I don't want her.'

"'You don't want her?'

"'I don't love her.'

"'You don't love her?'

"'Not in the least,' he replied, growing angry, perhaps at himself. 'What is she to me? Nothing. A very good missionary, no doubt; but *I* don't fancy woman-preachers. You may remember that *I* never gave in to her influence; *I* was never under her thumb. *I* was the only man in Little Fishing who cared nothing for her!'

"'And that is the secret of *her* liking,' murmured the Doctor. 'O woman! woman! the same the world over!'

"In the mean time the crowd had stood stupefied.

"'He does not love her!' they said to each other; 'he does not want her!'

"Andy's black eyes gleamed with joy; he swung himself up on to the platform. Mitchell stood there with face dark and disturbed, but he did not flinch. Whatever his faults, he was no hypocrite. 'I must leave this to-night,' he said to himself, and turned to go. But quick as a flash our Lady sprang from her knees and threw herself at his feet. 'You are going,' she cried. 'I heard what you said,—you don't love me! But take me with you,—oh, take me with you! Let me be your servant—your slave—anything—anything, so that I am not parted from you, my lord and master, my only, only love!'

"She clasped his ankles with her thin, white hands, and laid her face on his dusty shoes.

"The whole audience stood dumb before this manifestation of a great love. Enraged, bitter, jealous as was each heart, there was not a man but would at that moment have sacrificed his own love that she might be blessed. Even Mitchell, in one of those rare spirit-flashes when the soul is shown bare in the lightning, asked himself, 'Can I not love her?' But the soul answered, 'No.' He stooped, unclasped the clinging hands, and turned resolutely away.

"'You are a fool,' said the Doctor. 'No other woman will ever love you as she does.'

"'I know it,' replied Mitchell.

"He stepped down from the platform and crossed the church, the silent crowd making a way for him as he passed along; he went out into the sunshine, through the village, down towards the beach,—they saw him no more.

"The Lady had fainted. The men bore her back to the lodge and tended her with gentle care one week—two weeks—three weeks. Then she died.

"They were all around her; she smiled upon them all, and called them all by name, bidding them farewell. 'Forgive me,' she whispered to the Doctor. The Nightingale sang a hymn, sang as he had never sung before. Black Andy knelt at her feet. For some minutes she lay scarcely breathing; then suddenly she opened her fading eyes. 'Friends,' she murmured, 'I am well punished. I thought myself holy,—I held myself above my kind,—but God has shown me I am the weakest of them all.'

"The next moment she was gone.

"The men buried her with tender hands. Then, in a kind of blind fury against Fate, they tore down her empty lodge and destroyed its every fragment; in their grim determination they even smoothed over the ground and planted shrubs and bushes, so that the very location might be lost. But they did not stay to see the change. In a month the camp broke up of itself, the town was abandoned, and the island deserted for good and all; I doubt whether any of the men ever came back or even stopped when passing by. Probably I am the only one. Thirty years ago,—thirty years ago!"

"That Mitchell was a great fool," I said, after a long pause. "The Doctor was worth twenty of him; for that matter, so was Black Andy. I only hope the fellow was well punished for his stupidity."

"He was."

"Oh, you kept track of him, did you?"

"Yes. He went back into the world, and the woman he loved repulsed him a second time, and with even more scorn than before."

"Served him right."

"Perhaps so; but after all, what could he do? Love is not made to order. He loved one, not the other; that was his crime. Yet,—so strange a creature is man,—he came back after thirty years, just to see our Lady's grave."

"What! Are you"—

"I am Mitchell,—Reuben Mitchell."

—1874